Your Limitless Pet Business

Grow an Easy, Fun and Wildly Profitable Pet Business Online

Karly Edwards

Your Limitless Pet Business
Grow an Easy, Fun, and Wildly Profitable Pet Business Online
© 2024 Karly Edwards

All rights reserved. No part of this book may be reproduced, stored in a retrieval system or transmitted in any form or by any means (electronic, mechanical, photocopy, recording, scanning or other) except for brief quotations in critical reviews or articles, without the prior written permission of the publisher.

ISBN: 9781068307300 Paperback

Published by: Inspired By Publishing

The strategies in this book are presented primarily for enjoyment and educational purposes. Every effort has been made to trace copyright holders and obtain their permission for the use of copyright material.

The information and resources provided in this book are based upon the authors' personal experiences. Any outcome, income statements or other results, are based on the authors' experiences and there is no guarantee that your experience will be the same. There is an inherent risk in any business enterprise or activity and there is no guarantee that you will have similar results as the author as a result of reading this book.

The author reserves the right to make changes and assumes no responsibility or liability whatsoever on behalf of any purchaser or reader of these materials.

Acknowledgements

Writing a book is no easy feat, and I wouldn't have been able to get this book out into the world without the support and inspiration I've received along the way. My deepest thanks go to my partner Chris – the one who always believes in me, even when I don't. The one who tells me every day how amazing I am, even after I've brushed off his compliments for the millionth time. I wouldn't be where I am today without his unwavering support and belief in my ability to do anything and everything.

A special thanks goes to four roborovski hamsters named Squeak, Dr. Puff Bum, Bruce and Lord Fido Huffington, who are sadly no longer with us. Most importantly, a huge thank you to my magnificent miniature schnauzer, Loki. They are the inspiration behind the business I've built and the people I choose to work with. Animal lovers are the best people, and I'm beyond grateful I get to work with other humans who are as passionate about pets as I am. It makes every day a joy to serve.

Thank you to the beta readers who took the time to read this book in its raw form, and provided valuable feedback to make it better. It's always nerve-racking handing over a labour of love to those first readers, but your kind words and encouragement made the process much easier. Thank you.

A big thank you to the team at Inspired By Publishing. Publishing and launching a new book can be daunting, but your expertise and support along the way have kept my sanity and produced a book I'm proud to put my name to.

Lastly, my greatest thanks goes to the thousands of pet professionals in my community who have followed, supported and worked with me over the years. Helping you grow your own limitless pet businesses is what gets me out of bed in the morning. You're the reason I show up every day and create solutions that make your business more successful and easier to run. Thank you for being in my world.

Foreword

In today's fast-paced digital world, the pet industry is thriving with innovation and opportunities. Pet guardians are no longer just customers – they're individuals seeking guidance, a deeper connection and expert care for their beloved companions. This industry transformation means that, more than ever, pet business owners can carve out a rewarding, flexible and incredibly profitable niche by serving this growing audience in meaningful ways.

This is where Your Limitless Pet Business: Grow an Easy, Fun, and Wildly Profitable Pet Business Online by Karly Edwards comes into play. With over 15 years as a dog trainer and behaviourist, I found this book to be an invaluable resource, brimming with fresh perspectives, transformative strategies and practical steps that anyone in the pet industry can benefit from.

Karly's approach is both refreshing and revolutionary. She understands that success in this field requires more than just technical know-how – it demands a blend of passion, commitment and above all, a positive and growth-oriented mindset. In her book, Karly not only shares the tactics for thriving in the digital age, but also emphasises the importance of personal development. This dual focus on both business strategy and mindset is a game-changer for anyone who wants to achieve sustainable success and personal fulfilment. It's not just about hitting financial targets, but about building a business that brings joy and fulfilment while helping pets and their guardians lead better lives.

What makes *Your Limitless Pet Business* stand out is Karly's accessible, step-by-step approach to teaching her strategies. Whether you're a seasoned pro in the pet industry or just starting out, her insights are easy to follow and remarkably actionable. There's no fluff or overcomplication here. Every chapter is designed to guide you through key areas, everything from understanding your target audience and setting up an effective online presence to crafting engaging content and fostering a loyal community of clients. She takes complex marketing concepts and distils them into straightforward, practical methods that are manageable and effective for any pet business.

A truly noteworthy aspect of Karly's guidance is her holistic approach. She doesn't just tell you to set up a website or post on social media; she encourages you to consider how each of these actions can align with your values and vision. This book offers not only the "what" and "how," but also the "why" behind each strategy. In doing so, Karly creates a blueprint for building a business that's uniquely yours – a business that feels less like work and more like a natural extension of your passion and purpose.

Beyond business development, Karly also focuses on areas often overlooked by business owners: mindset and personal growth. By honing in on the importance of self-belief, resilience and a growth mindset, Karly reminds us that success isn't just about external strategies, but also about our inner attitude and perspective. Her insights on overcoming self-doubt, handling setbacks and maintaining motivation resonate deeply and will help you become both a better business owner and a better version of yourself. Through these reflections, Karly reminds us that building a successful business is as much a personal journey as it is a professional one.

I can personally attest to the power of Karly's strategies. I thought I had seen and learned it all, but Karly's insights offered fresh, inspiring and highly practical ways to adapt and grow in today's online landscape. Her focus on working smarter rather than harder, on harnessing your unique strengths, and on building authentic connections with your audience has changed my perspective on what it means to run a pet business today.

At its core, this book is a call to embrace the limitless possibilities available to pet business owners in the online world. It's about more than just making a profit; it's about making an impact, building a brand that reflects who you are and creating a sustainable and enjoyable business. Karly's passion for helping others succeed shines through every chapter, and her strategies have the potential to empower anyone willing to put the time and effort in.

So, if you're ready to take your pet business to new heights, embrace digital growth and make a meaningful difference in the lives of pets and their guardians, you're in the right place. Karly Edwards has created a blueprint that will guide you, challenge you, and, most importantly, inspire you to realise the full potential of your limitless pet business. Enjoy the journey, take action on each step and watch as your pet business becomes everything you've dreamed it could be.

Rachel Woollven
Dog Trainer and Behaviourist at Canine Connection

Contents

Introduction	1
Chapter 1 - Adopt an Unshakeable Mindset	7
Chapter 2 - Introducing the EASE System	17
Chapter 3 - Nail the Business Foundations	25
Chapter 4 - Aligning Your Services with You	47
Chapter 5 - The Mothership of Your Business	61
Chapter 6 - Online Marketing Simplified	71
Chapter 7 - Being Visible on Social Media	95
Chapter 8 - Achieve More in Half the Time	107
Chapter 9 - Designing Your Ideal Life	121
Chapter 10 - The Anti-Hustle Way	129
About the Author	139
Reviews	140
References	142

Introduction

I've written this book to both inspire and guide you on your journey to building the pet business of your dreams. After reading this book, I want you to get excited about the limitless possibilities in front of you. I want you to let go of all the confusion and frustration that might be plaguing your mind, and walk away with renewed optimism that running a business can be fun and easy. Along the way there will be hard truths, and sometimes, uncomfortable lessons to learn. Above all else, I want to gift you a tangible plan you can put into action. And not next week, not next year, but *today*. Speedy, imperfect action is the key to unlocking the success you desire. Make a commitment and tell yourself that this is the moment you make game-changing shifts in your life and pet business.

I've been in business since 2013 and I'm a certified business strategist. I've grown my successful business as the go-to pet business coach and built another venture from the ground up. Today, I've served thousands of pet professionals through my online courses, memberships and group programmes. The reason this book exists is because it's the information I wish I'd had when I first started. I'm on a mission to simplify business and online marketing for others in the pet industry, and I hope this goes a long way to achieving that.

I'm not going to lie and say the money always flowed and everything was always easy. For the first six years of my business, there were a bunch of tears and meltdowns. For years, nobody knew I existed, because I let my fears take the driving seat. During those six years, my income hovered at an infuriating £13,000 a year, even though I worked 50+ hours a week trying to do all of the things. Clearly it was all the wrong things.

As a super introvert with a few health conditions (PMS, IBS, dermatitis and chronic back pain) I've always been happiest out of the spotlight. I still am. But now I have a strategy that aligns with both my personality and energy levels. A strategy that allows me to make heaps of money while giving me the freedom I need to breathe. Now I work no more than 20 hours a week, and I have the means to step away from the business when I need to. In fact, I take multiple holidays abroad each year. I can spend big when I want to, like building a large extension of my home, and never second-guess myself about purchase decisions. This isn't a bragging exercise. I say this because I want you to understand what's possible for you.

I know that business and marketing can feel scary, frustrating and complicated. I speak with so many pet business owners who feel it's their biggest weak point. They're unsure about their next steps to grow and scale. They're often worried about putting themselves out there because they fear what others might say. They proclaim that they're terrible at writing or they're just no good at all this online stuff. They're keeping themselves small and broke because they make excuse after excuse about why they can't show up as their most powerful selves. Honestly, I get it. After all, you created your business to change the lives of pets and their people, not to be stuck behind a computer screen trying to get your head around all the different strategies and tech.

I'm here to change that.

I want you to have a business that totally lights you up. When you get up in the morning, I want you to be buzzing about what you're going to do that day. I want you to be truly and deeply in love with the work you do. I want you to have a predictable, repeatable way to bring in the leads and clients you need. I want you to make the money you want and live the lifestyle that speaks to your heart.

This is about growing your business in a way that aligns with *you*. Forget about what everyone else is saying you should be doing. No, you don't need to post 10 Instagram reels every day with you pointing and dancing. (Urgh, don't even!). You don't even need to use social media for your business if you don't want to. There are plenty of other ways to get your business booked out with five-star customers.

When you've finished this book, I want you to be excited, confident and crystal clear on your next steps. I want you to hold in your hands your perfectly aligned strategy that's going to get you to the heady success you know you're meant for. I want you to take that strategy and start putting it into action so you can attract the leads and customers you desire. Ultimately, I want you to shift your mindset to embody more ease and fun in both your life and your business.

I hope that by the end of this book, you will see how powerful and limitless you truly are.

What It Means to Be a Limitless Pet Business Owner

You may be wondering what it actually means to be limitless. I'll break this down for you into three simple areas so you can easily understand what it means to embrace the limitless you.

You Know Your Income Is Limitless

You don't subscribe to the idea that there's a cap on your earning potential. You know that your income has no ceiling, and isn't determined just because Sally the dog trainer down the road is fully booked and earns X amount. You have an unwavering belief that there is always more, and that there's an unlimited number of ways you can make money. If you want to make £5,000 a month, that's available to you. If you want to make £100,000 a month, you can. There's money in this world that's ready for taking. If you want it, you have to claim it.

You Know Your Impact Is Limitless

As a Limitless Pet Business, you have a calling to change the lives of hundreds, thousands, if not millions of pets and their people. You have an extraordinary message to share with the world. You don't let your fears stand in the way of getting your message in front of the people who need to hear it. You are here to serve and transform lives. You're not confined to hours available in the day or the area you work in. You know that your impact can touch people and pets across the entire world and you're ready to leave a legacy.

You Know Your Freedom Is Limitless

You know that while you love your business and the clients you work with, life is made for living. You give yourself permission to look after yourself. You give your mind and body exactly what it needs so you can show up as the best version of yourself. You don't feel trapped by your business. You have solid boundaries and support in place that allow you to step back when you need it.

I realise that all this talk of being limitless can feel like a tall order. You might be thinking, "Yeah Karly, that sounds great. But that's so far from my reality I could cry a river of tears!" It might seem impossible right now, and your mind may have gone straight to the question, "But how!?" Well, that's exactly what I'm here to show you.

I'm not going to claim that my own life and business are perfect in all three areas. If we can agree on one thing, it's that life is an ongoing journey of learning and development. Yes, I make mistakes. There are still moments where I work too much. I have wild ebbs and flows in my energy and mood, which makes me want to hide away sometimes. I'm often seduced by the idea of hitting the next big money goal. But we're not looking for perfection here. We're looking for massive progress in the right direction.

If you have a fire in your belly to change your life and make a difference in this world, it can be yours. Anyone can be limitless in income, impact and freedom. And that "anyone" includes *you*. I know that's you, because you wouldn't have chosen to read this book otherwise.

As we go on this journey together, I'll share both practical strategy and insightful lessons gained from my own experience. You might feel some resistance towards the lessons I share. Those mind monkeys may jump on your shoulder and whisper, "I can't do that." For the sake of your success and happiness, come into this book with an open mind and a willingness to make big changes. It might just be the turning point that shapes a whole new world for you.

This book comes with a handy digital workbook you can fill in to implement what you learn along the way. You'll find the workbook at: www.karlyedwards.com/workbook

Chapter 1
Adopt an Unshakeable Mindset

You can have all the perfect business strategies in the world, but without a strong mindset, it will always be an uphill battle. Even with a fancy website, professional branding and a big audience, a weak mindset will always find a way to sabotage your success.

We can stay stuck at the same level for years if we focus only on the strategies and tactics, especially if we're constantly jumping from one thing to the next. Instead, we must allow ourselves to go inward, often. We must bring awareness to all our thoughts, feelings, beliefs and fears. Without reflection, we're doing business with our eyes closed.

You are the conductor of your life and business. You're a living, breathing human with unique wants and needs. Your mind needs nurturing just as your business does. All those negative thoughts and feelings want to be heard. They want to have a voice. It does us no good when we choose to ignore them and treat them as if they don't exist. I'll be honest with you, working on your mindset isn't always easy. Sometimes it'll feel uncomfortable to confront them. Sometimes it'll leave you a weeping mess on the floor. But on the other side of that, you'll find a new version of you.

You'll be far more aware of who you are and you'll be ready to embrace your next level.

We all have phases when the negative mind chatter feels out of control. It can last days, weeks, sometimes months. The negative self-talk can be brutal. "I'm worthless, nobody likes me, I'm not good enough, I'm too fat, I'm not clever enough to do that...." It can be relentless and debilitating.

Other times, you'll feel like you're smashing it and ready to take on the world. I'm sure you know what I'm talking about here. Only by being aware of these inner voices and showing them love and understanding can you quieten them and reduce their control over you. This is how you reduce the severity and frequency of those low moments, so you can quickly pick yourself up and get back on the train to winning at life.

The sad thing is, many people surrender to their own fears and limiting beliefs. Something won't work out as they expected, they'll get a refund request or someone will leave a bad review. Most people will see the first hint of trouble as a sign that they're not cut out for life in business. Just like that, they've shut up shop and gone back to working for someone else. By god, I do not want that for you.

You have an incredible service to offer the world. You are valuable, needed and wanted. Are you going to let your self-criticism stand in the way of changing your own life and the lives of pets and their people? It's your responsibility to showcase the amazing work you do so other people can benefit. It would be selfish to keep all that talent to yourself, don't you think?

Get curious about every single negative thought that enters your mind. Ask yourself: "Why do I think that? Where did it come from?" I love playing this game so I can learn more about myself. It will often bring me back to a memory where that belief was formed. It could be an experience that happened to me or something someone said to me. It could even be something I've just made up and accepted as truth.

Everything that happens in our lives shapes how we feel about ourselves and the world. It shapes all of our thoughts, beliefs and the actions we take. Pretty crazy how much power our experiences hold over us, huh? Then ask yourself, "Is this really true, or is this someone else's mindset block I've taken on as my own?" I can almost guarantee that's exactly what's happened. In fact, let's have a quick look at some common mindset blocks that can hold us back.

"I'm Not Good Enough"

Not-enoughness and imposter syndrome are the biggest mindset hurdles I hear from my clients and the wider community. Maybe you feel you're not qualified enough. You see your competitors and get that horrible feeling that they're better than you. Or maybe you don't feel ready yet. This belief can lead to sabotaging behaviours like hiding away because you're too afraid to be called out as a fraud. You don't put yourself out there in fear that other people will say you're wrong. Or, you stay stuck in a perpetual cycle of learning your trade.

You buy course after course to further your knowledge in your area of expertise, but never actually invest in how to actually grow your business and make money from it.

I hear you. This belief has been a running theme in my life for as long as I can remember. It came directly from my life experiences and is something I continue to work on to this day.

Sometimes, you can never eliminate these beliefs entirely. Every time you reach a new level in business, they'll come back to challenge you again. You'll be thinking, "I thought I'd dealt with this!" But there it'll be, and you'll need to do the inner work again to let it go. My feelings of not-enoughness were born from many moments throughout my life.

When I was 13 years old, I had two best friends who unexpectedly turned on me and bullied me for the rest of the school year. To this day, I still have no idea why they did that.

My boss in my first ever grown-up job was an erratic and impatient man. He was often inappropriate and unreasonable, too. I worked my socks off for very little pay, and one day, during one of his tantrums, he said four little words to me: "This isn't good enough." These words often come back to haunt me, because my brain turned them into, "*You're* not good enough." When I got home to my flat that night, I sat on the edge of my bed and cried my eyes out.

My first serious boyfriend left me to pursue a relationship with another girl in my friendship circle. (Funnily, they never did get together.) Soon after we broke up, he started chasing me, asking me to come back to him. Clearly, he didn't know that I'm not the forgiving type after a betrayal.

I stayed with my next boyfriend for eight years, only for him to break up with me to play the field. Kudos to him for being honest with me. It still left me utterly crushed at the time though.

Boyfriend number three cheated on me after we lived and worked together for a year. It was a messy breakup. At the time, the only logical place I could turn to was my family home with my dad. I remember calling him while sitting in my car, surrounded by my belongings. I told him I'd broken up with my boyfriend and asked if I could move back in. I wasn't prepared for his answer. He said "no" because his girlfriend at the time didn't want me to ruin the newly fitted carpet in my childhood bedroom.

It's never pleasant to relive any of these memories. Each one has contributed to an overall heaviness of not-enoughness throughout my life, each one building on the last. It's taken a lot of internal reflection to forgive, let go and move past them so I can be the best version of myself.

You have to believe in your heart that you are good enough, just as you are. If other people can be successful, why not you? You don't need to have all the qualifications, win all the awards or take that other dog-training course. Pet parents need you and the experience you have right now. You can always develop your expertise over time. It's time to show them exactly what you can do to help them, today.

Fear of Failure

There will be many challenges and failures along the way. I've had plenty. There isn't a business owner out there who hasn't. You'll create a new service and no one will buy. You'll share a post on social media and not get a single like or comment. You'll receive complaints from people who aren't happy with your service. You'll set plenty of goals and not hit them. It happens. It's a rite of passage. I spent three months creating my first online course and another two months promoting it. After all that effort, only one person bought it. I made exactly £247 from five months' worth of work. If I'd thrown in the towel after that failure, I wouldn't have gone on to sell thousands of courses today.

We're great at sharing the highlight reels online, not so much the raw and gritty behind-the-scenes. Seeing all this success around us can make us feel like big fat failures. Never compare yourself to someone else's 15-year milestone when you're only three years in. Many attempts and failures have gone into their journey to get them to where they are today. You'll get there too, but it's pointless comparing apples to pears. You have to put the blinkers on and focus on yourself and your business. You'll fail a bunch of times and learn along the way. It's part of doing business.

Fear of Success

I've never really had a fear of failure. But a fear of success? Absolutely. Oftentimes we're most worried about what that success will mean for us. We create a mindset block around it and end up sabotaging ourselves. We think, "More success usually comes with more responsibility."

In the early stages of my business, I let the fear of success stop me from growing because I was scared I'd lose my freedom.

After all, if more people buy, that's more people to serve. With more people to serve, that's more work on my shoulders.

As someone who's massively introverted and isn't in the best state of health, this concern stayed with me for years. I want and need space in my life, which is the very reason why I've chosen the business model I have today.

We have so many more opportunities available to us now. Opportunities that just 20 years ago wouldn't have been possible. These days you can grow a wildly successful business and have tons of free time, too. You don't have to compromise anymore. Now, you can sell an online dog training course to someone in another country. You could write a book and reach millions of pet parents all over the world. You could hold a group workshop online and sell it at £10 to hundreds of pet parents. You can build success in any way that works for you. We're limited only by our own imagination.

Without being self-aware and letting go of the limiting beliefs that don't serve you, you'll always stay stuck exactly where you are. While it can be scary to shine a light on them, it'll do you a world of good in the long run.

This is a tiny snapshot of what it means to develop an unshakeable mindset. While it is instrumental for your success, this is not a mindset book and I won't pretend to be an expert.

I encourage you to continuously develop your knowledge in this area.

It has been fundamental for me on my own business journey and it'll do the same for you. I'm giving an honourable mention to Lenka Lutonska and Denise Duffield-Thomas for their incredible work in this field. I wouldn't be where I am today without their support. Follow them and absorb everything they have to offer.

Exercise: Uncovering Your Mind Monkeys

In your ready-made workbook, jot down any negative thoughts, beliefs or fears you have about yourself and your ability to be successful. Write each of them down as a simple sentence in a bulleted list first. Then go deeper and give each one the time and attention they deserve. Fully offload all your thoughts and feelings around each belief. There's incredible power in awareness.

This is an ongoing process and you'll come across your negative thought patterns all the time. The key is becoming aware of them so you can address them as they arise. Get it all out so you can see it for what it is. Your fears and limiting beliefs will be unique to you, but here are a few common examples to get you started.

- I'm not good enough because…

- I can't be successful because…

- I have to work really hard if I want to make more money…

- I'm too old, young, fat, ugly, weird to be successful…

- I can't be visible because…

Tune into your inner critic on a regular basis and make friends with her. They are the key to unlocking the best version of you.

Grab your workbook below.

www.karlyedwards.com/workbook

Chapter 2
Introducing the EASE System

We can be great at overcomplicating business. We can throw out too many different services to try and please everyone. We feel we need to be everywhere online, with Facebook pages, Instagram, Pinterest, TikTok, email, blogs, podcasts, YouTube and Twitter all taking up digital and mental bandwidth. We sometimes try to do all the menial tasks ourselves, like booking people in, sending invoices manually, sending individual contracts and emails, updating our website or managing our inbox. I'm just touching the surface here, but it's *a lot* for just one person to handle.

I remember I was pretty clueless in the early stages of my business. I was fresh out of a full-time job working as the Marketing Executive for a software company. I was good at my job, but day-to-day I was just following orders. I didn't make the big decisions in the business, I only reported directly to the big boss. So, once I started working for myself, there was a humongous learning curve. There was no one to hold me accountable for the work I was doing, no one to tell me what needed to be done. I spent the best part of the first five years in business messing around on my laptop and taking naps at 11am every day.

As I wasn't making much money at the time, I'd waste hundreds of hours hunting down free solutions for the things my business needed. Instead of hiring a web designer, I found a free crappy WordPress theme and learnt how to develop it myself. Instead of paying for an email marketing system, I wasted hours researching the free options that would give me what I needed. Instead of paying for a social media scheduler, I surrendered to sharing all my posts manually every day.

So many of us put our sanity on the line and waste so much time because we don't seek the help we need and are too afraid to invest in our future.

There are easier ways to grow your pet business, and it often pays to put some skin in the game. It's like a big old signal to the Universe that you're serious about your business and that you're here to play! I'm not saying business is always a total breeze, otherwise everyone would be doing it. You can make it so much easier on yourself, though. That's why I developed the EASE System.

It simplifies business and marketing for pet professionals so you only focus on the right things. This is about letting go of what doesn't serve you and doubling down on what will grow the pet business of your dreams. Ready to learn this four-step system?

E Stands for Enterprise

Your business is your Enterprise. How your ideal customers perceive you is directly linked to how you present yourself online. Your online presence is all-important. It's what encourages your perfect people to follow everything you put out there. It's what makes them excited about being a part of your community. It's what compels them to reach out and say, "Take my money, you're the perfect person for me!" But before you start mindlessly shouting about your business online, we need to set the foundations first.

The foundations are your businesses' true north, and that's what this Enterprise step is all about. It's what guides everything you do and say. I'm a little embarrassed to admit that I didn't take this work seriously until I was seven years into my business.

Turns out, being open to working with anyone with a pulse and having about as much personality as a cucumber sandwich online really doesn't invite "work with me!" vibes.

We don't want a business that's trying to attract every single pet parent. We don't want a business that sounds like everyone else. You need to be crystal-clear on who you want to attract, what makes you unique and what values you stand for, as well as your messaging, positioning and tone. Then, you need to be able to package all that up to showcase how amazing you truly are. No pressure then! Good thing I'll be showing you how to do all of that in this book.

A Stands for Assets

Assets is just another word for your business model. These are the services or products you offer that will be the painkiller solution to your ideal customers' problems. It's crucial that you are head-over-heels in love with what you do. That you wake up in the morning and are so pumped to be offering your services to the world. You have to be unapologetically giddy about the solutions you provide, otherwise, what's the point? If you're not excited, you won't be able to talk about your offerings with enthusiasm. If you can't do that, how do you expect your potential customers to be enthused about investing in you?

This was the biggest mistake I made. For years, I offered services that weren't in alignment with my personality and energy levels. At the time, I offered done-for-you copywriting and content strategy. I managed other businesses' social media accounts. I wrote blog posts, press releases, websites and leaflets. Every day, I'd drag myself out of bed and begrudgingly tap away at my laptop for 10 hours, all while I clock-watched and waited for the day to end. It was misery.

That's no way to live. It was a magical day when I discovered passive income. Today, I only work with people through my online courses, memberships, digital resources and group programmes. This is what has allowed me to create the success and freedom I have today. You don't have to walk the same path as me, but you do have to be a hundred per cent behind your services.

S Stands for Strategy

Strategy is everything in business. It's the roadmap that guides you from where you are now to where you want to be. I see too many pet pros blindly floating about their business and wondering why it isn't working out the way they'd hoped. You need a strategy, my friend!

Your strategy starts with a simple goal. What do you want to achieve this time next year? The most important goal is your money goal. Do you want to make £30,000, £100,000 or maybe even a million this year? Figure out what you need to make to live the life you want, then form a strategy you can follow that will get you there.

The "how" is always the most difficult part though, right? We can get so caught up in all the different ways to bring new leads and customers into our businesses that we're left feeling confused and overwhelmed by it all. You don't have to be on every platform to hit your goals. You don't have to do things that make your skin crawl just because you've seen it work for someone else.

Here's what's most important: You form a simple strategy that feels good for you and delivers results. Then you repeat it, again and again and again.

When my clients first come to me, they often worry about the strategy. They're worried about the amount of time it might take when they're already spinning so many plates. They're worried that they might have to do something they don't want to. They worry they'll put in the effort and it won't make a single difference to their business success.

Good thing I do things differently around here. Strategy alignment means a strategy that suits you. It feels achievable and sustainable. Which means you'll be far more likely to stick with it for the long term. Consistency creates engaged audiences. An engaged audience leads to more customers for you.

E Stands for Engine

An Engine is the system you plug into your business that makes it considerably easier to run day-to-day. Systems and automation are the beating heart of your business. It's how you empower your business to operate without you. It's how you can take back control of your time and claim more freedom for yourself. We don't need to be actively involved in every tiny detail of our businesses.

You shouldn't be doing absolutely everything with your own two hands. There are a finite number of hours in the day. If your time and attention are taken up by manually booking people in or sending invoices, that's less time you have to make more sales or serve more clients. It's not productive and will limit your success.

Technology is a wonderful thing. There are so many tools out there that can quickly take tasks off our plates. This can give you more time to market yourself to bring in more money, or it can give you more time to indulge in some YOU time. For years, I was a slave to my business. Please don't make the same mistakes I did.

Remember when I mentioned how I avoided investing in anything? It took me the longest time to realise it's totally OK and more than worth it to spend a measly £8 a month on a booking system. I soon realised this decision saved me hours of back-and-forth emails to clients every month – time I could then spend writing blog posts or email campaigns to attract new clients. I now spend £10,000+ on tools, coaching and advertising every year to grow my business, and it's been money well spent to get me to where I am today.

The EASE System is about building your business on your terms. It covers the fundamentals you need to grow and scale the pet business of your dreams. It's the blueprint you need to make more money and embody that perfect work/life balance. This is all about empowering you to start living the lifestyle you've been craving for too long. So let's dig a little deeper, shall we?

Chapter 3
Nail the Business Foundations

Don't skip the basics. This work may not be sexy – it may even be frustrating or confronting at times – but give it the attention it needs. I often see too many pet business owners jumping headfirst into putting themselves out there without doing the background work first. They throw up a website without giving it much thought or they start mindlessly sharing on social media, then wondering why no one's buying from them. We need to clarify a few foundations first before we start doing any of that.

Your Big Vision

Your pathway to success all starts with your big vision. This is your wonderfully vivid brainchild of the life you want to lead. Where do you want to be in 1, 5 and 10 years? Do you know, down to the tiny details, what that looks like for you? If not, it's time to start dreaming! Without knowing exactly what kind of business and life you want to have, there's no motivation to make it happen.

When the end goal is unclear, how do you know what you're working towards and what steps you need to take to get there? The short answer: You don't.

That's why you need to use the incredible power of your own imagination to dream it up in your mind. Connect with your inner daydreamer and consider what's important to you. Dig deep to uncover, without limits, without all your mental baggage and limiting beliefs, what would be your ideal life. Then connect with that big vision, every single day.

Find a quiet five minutes in your day to close your eyes and tune into the future you, the one that has everything she desires. See yourself living that life and feel all the emotions wash over you as you put yourself in the shoes of this future you. This is important, because the more you can embody future you in the here and now, the more it is brought into your current reality. Read this paragraph again and let that sink in.

I haven't always been an ambitious person. After working various jobs since the age of 13, somewhere along the way, I knew I wanted to work for myself. For years, I didn't really have big goals. I wouldn't dream about having a big house, a fancy car or going on holidays to 5-star resorts. I just knew that

I had a problem with authority and I wanted to make my own way in life.

However, this breezy attitude always kept me in the slow lane in business. We need a vision to fuel our ambition. Without it, you'll always make an excuse for tolerating exactly where you are. A clear dream puts a fire in your belly to go after your ideal life. But you have to know precisely what you desire first.

Once you've identified what your big vision is, create a visual representation so you can remind yourself every day. I love dream boards for this very purpose. You can use pictures and words to sum up your big vision in one image. You can hang this up on a board in your workspace, or as I have, save it to the desktop background on your computer. Every time I log in, it's right there to remind me why I'm doing this thing we call business. When times are tough and we feel like jacking it all in, this will be the anchor you need to keep moving forward.

Exercise: Creating Your Big Vision

When creating your big vision, we need to break this down into two key areas: your business and your personal life. To support you in creating your big vision, use the questions below to get you started. Use the workbook I've prepared for you to start dreaming up your ideal life. Don't hold back.

Your Personal Life

Where do you live? What are all the features of the house you live in? Who are you with? What kind of relationship do you have with your partner/family/kids/pets/friends? How many holidays do you take a year? Where do you go on holiday? What kind of car do you have? Do you have any hobbies? How much time do you have to spend with friends and family? What kind of things do you do together? Do you have an exercise routine? If so, what is it? What kind of food do you eat? How much sleep do you get?

Your Business Life

How much money do you make a year? How many hours do you work a week? Where do you work? How do you work with pet parents? What kind of services do you offer? Do you have a team around you? If so, what does that look like? How many pet parents have you worked with? How many people do you have in your wider community online? Have you won any awards? What kind of influence and standing do you hold in your field?

Plan out your future life down to the minute detail. The more granular you can get the better. Then, take your mind to the future you for a few minutes every day.

Grab your workbook below.

www.karlyedwards.com/workbook

Your Ideal Customer

Who do you want to work with? Sounds like a simple enough question, but we need to have the highest level of clarity about your ideal customer to be able to draw in your perfect people. We're not trying to be all things to everyone. If you are, your message won't speak directly to anyone and you'll forever struggle to attract the customers you want. You must know your ideal customer intimately. You need to know their biggest pain points and desires, and how the services we offer will be the only solution to their current woes.

There are three primary levels to identifying your ideal customer. Firstly, we need to understand the surface-level details of who they are. I'm sure you've heard about demographics before and you've probably fleshed out a few ideas. Demographics is essentially information about your ideal client, such as:

- Where they live
- How old they are
- What gender they are
- If they're married
- If they have kids
- What pets they have
- Where they work
- How much money they make

- What kind of books, magazines or information they consume

With demographics, we're starting to paint a clear picture of a specific person and how they live their life. You may be able to gather some of this data from your website analytics or from social media insights. I often like to take this one step further though and ask my audience directly.

You'll get way more clarity by opening up a dialogue with your existing clients or audience. You can either post a question for them on social media or do it through email. Alternatively, you can send a personal invite to chat with them on the phone or through Zoom.

With the second level, we're going deeper into your ideal customer's problems and what really matters to them.

You may have done some work around this too, but it's important we don't brush over this step. One of the most fundamental elements of being in business is being able to identify and understand your customer's biggest problems and provide the best solution that will meet them where they're at.

Here we want to answer questions like:

- What are your ideal customer's ultimate goals?
- What are their values?

What challenges does your ideal customer face on a daily basis?

What are their biggest pain points?

What are their dreams and desires?

How do you help solve their problems and fulfil their desires?

Why does your ideal customer buy from you?

What do they love about you?

What don't they love about you?

What recently happened in their life that made your ideal customer search for information relating to the solution you offer?

What did your ideal customer already try that didn't work, and is the reason they're searching for your advice or solution?

When you're answering these questions, avoid putting one-sentence answers and try to be as detailed as possible. The more we know about your ideal customer, the better. Again, talking directly with your people will give you incredible insight here.

The third level is all about psychographics. These include the behaviours, habits, beliefs and traits of your ideal customer. Here we're lifting the lid on the type of personality you do and don't want to work with. Not all personalities mix, and that's totally OK.

Getting clear on your ideal customer's psychographics will help you spot the pet parents that are and aren't a good fit for your business. It'll help you quickly see any potential red flags before you start working with someone.

There's nothing worse than entering into a long-term commitment with a client, to then finding they're causing you stress for whatever reason. When your instinct is telling you something doesn't feel right, it's totally OK to say no.

Here we want to break this down into the characteristics you want to see and accept, alongside the characteristics you won't accept. If you dig deep enough, you can easily uncover 50 to 100 in each category. On the positive side, this might look like:

- Your ideal customer pays on time
- They arrive at their sessions on time
- They have a positive outlook on life
- They do the homework outside of sessions with you
- They're coachable and open to taking your advice on board
- They happily refer you to friends and family
- A force-free approach is important to them
- Their pet's happiness and welfare is their priority

On the negative side, the people you don't want to attract might be:

- Those who always pay late
- Those who arrive late to sessions or cancel last minute
- Those who have a negative attitude
- Those who don't take personal responsibility and never do their homework
- Those who constantly question or disregard your advice
- Those who resort to aversive techniques when they're not seeing the results they want quickly enough
- Those who punish their pet when they do something they don't like

Your ideal customer will constantly evolve over time, so it's important to revisit this work at least once a year. As you change and your business grows, you might change the requirements for your ideal customer. You might develop it further as you learn more about them, or you might pivot slightly.

Nothing is set in stone. You have the power to set the rules on who you do and don't want to work with at any time.

Exercise: Identifying Your Ideal Customer

In your workbook, start fleshing out your ideal customer. Remember to go deep on the three key areas:

- Demographics
- Their big problems and what matters to them
- Psychographics

Grab your workbook below.

www.karlyedwards.com/workbook

Your Core Values

Now that we know more about who your ideal customer is, we need to understand more about your business and what matters to you. We all have our own unique perspectives on the world. There are certain moral codes we hold that help shape who we are as people and business owners. Your core business values help define every action you should take in your business, from the way you treat your customers and wider community, to how you communicate with partners and as a team. Values are guiding beliefs that help everyone associated with your business function together as one.

We need core values to attract the right people. As humans, we're often drawn to brands with the same values as us. When your values are aligned with your customers, that's when beautiful relationships are formed. You get each other. You have the same perspectives, which makes those people far more likely to choose you. Having core values simplifies your decision making too. It's easier to make a decision when you know exactly what matters to your business. If an opportunity feels out of alignment with your core beliefs, you know when it's time to say no. Equally, when an opportunity is in alignment, it's easier to come to a confident yes.

Your values differentiate you from your competitors. They can be the reason someone decides to choose you over the next dog sitter, dog walker or dog trainer down the road. One of my biggest values is "freedom." It's important to me that I'm able to work on my terms, from wherever and whenever I want. My introverted brain and health challenges mean I need that space and time to breathe. I've grown my business in a way to allow that fully.

I talk about this value a lot in the content I share, and it's what attracts many of my ideal customers to me. They want more freedom in their lives too, and I have the solutions to show them how. One of my other core values is "security," across all aspects of life. Being secure financially, in my relationships and in my home is essential for me.

My life was on a rocky road for years when it came to security, which is why it's a priority for me today. Financial security is often important to the pet pros I work with too, which is why I teach them how to make more money and create recurring revenue.

You should aim for three to five core business values. To define your own values, you need to start by uncovering what matters to you. It always helps to start capturing your purpose – your big "why" for doing what you do. Your values should portray how you'll conduct your business and carry out that purpose.

Think about your life as a whole and what you stand for as a person. What are you passionate about? It can be tempting to look around and copy the values of other similar businesses. By all means, use them to inspire you – but there's no point trying to be someone else. You can't truly embody values and act on them with passion when they aren't your own.

To get your cogs turning, here are some core values to inspire you:

- Adventure – to have new and exciting experiences
- Caring – to care for others
- Compassion – to feel and act on concern for others
- Dependability – to be reliable and trustworthy
- Growth – to keep changing and growing
- Honesty – to be honest and truthful

- Knowledge – to learn and contribute valuable knowledge
- Tolerance – to accept and respect those who differ from us

On the flip side of this, you should also define the opposite. What are the things in life you stand against? What triggers you and causes a negative emotional response? These are the facts or situations you'd love to change about the world. When you use your passion in this way and share it in your messaging, it will further attract people who have the same viewpoints as you do.

For example, I have a deep, visceral reaction when I see people using aversive tools and techniques in the dog training world. Or any kind of animal cruelty, actually. It's why I only work with force-free pet businesses.

I'm passionate about helping ethical pet pros put themselves out there powerfully so they can impact more people and pets, and I use this in my messaging. Bad customer service is another big bugbear of mine. I can't tolerate businesses that make it so difficult to get support when you need it. It's why I prioritise my clients to ensure they feel truly held and supported in everything I do.

While you're defining your values, consider what you stand against too, so you can use it in the messaging you share.

Exercise: Identifying Your Core Values

In your workbook, start brainstorming a list of core values that really matter to you. Then based on your level of passion for each one, pull out three to five that will become your business values.

At the same time, brainstorm the situations in the world that tick you off. These will become the things you stand against that you can talk about with your wider audience.

Grab your workbook below.

www.karlyedwards.com/workbook

Your Unique Identifiers and Positioning

If someone asked you what makes you different from your competitors, would you be able to tell them in a few sentences? Oftentimes, pinning down our uniqueness is one of the biggest areas we struggle with as business owners. Sometimes we're simply unable to see how incredible we really are, while many of us have been conditioned to dim our light – by society or the people around us.

This can unconsciously create thought spirals in our mind that we've picked up from other people, like: "Don't shine too brightly," "It's not polite to brag," "It's not safe to stick out," "I don't want to attract unwanted attention." It's no wonder we suffer from an internal battle that's constantly trying to keep us small. You're an amazing individual who's gone through your own unique journey to get to where you are today. You just need to pull some of that out and shine a light on it so your customers can see it, too.

Your unique identifiers position you as the go-to solution for a specific problem. It's what connects your customers with you more deeply. There are lots of ways to solidify your uniqueness, but one of the easiest ways is to niche down, where you become known for a very specific area of expertise. That way, when a pet parent has a problem that you specialise in, they know exactly who to turn to.

Let's say you're a dog behaviourist and you're currently working with all kinds of dogs with all kinds of behaviour problems. When your potential customer is researching their options and you all look the same, you might have a one in four chance of getting booked. Instead, what if you specialise only in helping dogs who are reactive to other dogs outside the home? Now we're starting to become THE expert for that specific problem, which makes you a far more appealing option over the more generalised behaviourists. You could even take this one step further and niche down by specific breed too. Or let's say you're a dog walker. Maybe you niche in enrichment walks.

Instead of promoting generic group walks where you pound the streets in your area, you offer walks with scent games and light training to combine both physical and mental stimulation. Now there's a service my schnauzer Loki and I would get behind in a shot!

You'd be forgiven for thinking niching down will limit your client pool and potential income. You might think niching will mean fewer opportunities, customers and money in the bank. But in fact, the opposite happens. Sure, you do become the big fish in the lake, but that's far better than being a tiny fish in a massive ocean. Besides, as you become known as the go-to, you'll likely attract people wanting other services slightly outside your front-facing expertise too. Then it's up to you if you want to say yes to those opportunities or refer them to someone else.

If you'd rather not niche down, you can always communicate your uniqueness in other ways.

Your qualifications. Do you have a certain set of qualifications that set you apart from the rest?

Your life experiences. What's your backstory and life experiences that are relevant to the work you do today? How does that experience benefit your customer?

Your work experiences. What work experience do you have and how do you apply that to the work you do now?

Your business successes. What are the big successes in your business that add to your credibility? Do you have an incredibly high client success rate, have you won any awards?

Your results. What results or transformations do you create for your customers?

Your approach. Do you have a unique method, approach or process you provide in the work you do?

Your values. We've already looked at your core values in more detail, but this is another opportunity to put your flag in the sand and set yourself apart.

By answering these questions and looking at the facts in black and white, you'll no doubt uncover a range of unique identifiers you can shout about. Let's not forget too, *you* are unique. Your personality, energy, the way you present yourself – you are the biggest unique identifier. Just by being you, the right people will be drawn to you. Just by showing up and authentically sharing your message, people will be attracted to you as a person. There are pet parents out there right now who are waiting for you to come along and help them.

Because of who you are, *you* are the perfect person to help them. This is exactly why you need to be 100% confident, accepting and comfortable with who you are inside and out. Only when we love ourselves fully, can we show up in our full power and show others why they should love us too.

Exercise: Solidify Your Unique Identifiers

In your workbook, start brainstorming your unique identifiers. Ask yourself if there's an opportunity to niche either by breed or by the problem you solve. Capture your answers to the seven questions shared above, and reflect on how you can bring out more of you and your personality in the way you show up.

Grab your workbook below.

www.karlyedwards.com/workbook

Your Messaging

Your messaging is the way you communicate the value you provide to your audience and ideal customers. It's the core topics you talk about around your business. It's where you bring out your unique tone, phrases and personality in the content you share. It's how you build strong connections with the people you want to work with and how you inspire them to buy from you.

The topics, language, design, imagery and values you share, all tell a story of who you are as a business. When you package all of this up in a powerful way, it becomes your brand identity.

The pet parents that see it will either be drawn to it, or repelled by it. It's OK and good to polarise people in this way.

Remember, we're not trying to be all things to everyone. With a strong message, the right people will fall head over heels in love with what you have to offer. *That's* the people we want to attract.

A lot of this work follows on from the exercises we've already uncovered in the section above. A lot of the work you've already done will make up your messaging as a whole. We also need to be able to condense some of that down into a power statement that very quickly sums up who you help, the problem you solve and how you solve it. This can then be used on things like your social bios, business cards, email signature, opening statement on your website and more.

We also need to define the five to seven core topics that will make up your message. When we're sharing content online, we don't want to throw out the first thing that pops into our head.

Your online presence should be curated and defined by the core topics you want to become known for.

We can break this down into two categories:

Your Primary Message

Your primary message can be summed up in your power statement. It encapsulates, in a concise way, exactly who you help and how you help them. We want to bring out your uniqueness and give your customers a compelling reason to choose you. This is the very essence of what your business is about. Make it clear and enticing.

Your primary messaging is also the key topic(s) you'll talk about that relate to the services you provide. For example, if you're a dog trainer, your key topics may simply be puppy training and training for adolescent dogs. That's your main focus. Then you'll have many more subtopics within that which you can break down further in the content you share.

To give you an example from my own business, the core topics in my primary message include: business strategy, online marketing, creating passive and semi/passive income, and productivity and systems to save time. I don't veer away from my primary message, because that will dilute my impact. If you try to become known for too many things, you'll always be faced with a hard battle to the top.

Your Secondary Message

Your secondary messaging is often more personal. It leans more towards your beliefs and the things you stand for and against as an individual. Your secondary messaging is often what creates raving fans and loyal customers because they love and appreciate you as a person. We can draw on our values to help us define our secondary messaging. Think about three to five topics you can use here.

To give you an example from my own business, mine are: freedom lifestyle, introversion, dog mum life and no hustle culture. Within your core topics, you'll create content that perfectly reflects these perspectives and beliefs. So let's say I'm sharing content around the core topic: freedom lifestyle. I might share pictures of me on holiday and talk about how grateful I am to have a business that allows me to step away and travel when I want to. Or I might talk about the strategy I use that allows me to grow my business as an introvert. They lend more towards my passions and the personal side of who I am, but it all relates back to the business and how I can help my ideal people.

Exercise: Pinning Down Your Messaging

In your workbook, use this formula to create your own power statement:

We/I help .... who are struggling with ....
And want to .... through/by ....

Here's an example using the power statement formula:

I help busy schnauzer guardians who struggle with frustration and embarrassment from their dog's antics and want more calm at home and on walks, through my one-to-one training packages.

Then, brainstorm your core topics for your primary and secondary messaging and choose a handful from each that you want to become known for.

Grab your workbook below.

www.karlyedwards.com/workbook

Chapter 4
Aligning Your Services with You

Being in total alignment with the services you offer is key to a sustainable business. If you don't love what you do, somewhere along the line something's going to break. You might wake up one morning and think, "Enough is enough. I just can't go on like this, dammit!" That breaking point might come from boredom. It could come from exhaustion. It might be fuelled by a persistent feeling of never earning enough for the effort you're putting in. We need to be in this for the long term. I know you know that it takes some time and effort to grow a business.

Success doesn't happen overnight, and we need to be able to talk about the services we offer with excitement for years to come. This means you must have an unwavering passion for the work you do, and it should never leave you feeling drained or burnt out. You also deserve to be well compensated for the solutions you provide.

There are many different business models and services you could provide in your pet business. What's most important is finding the one that most aligns with your personality and energy levels. Just because a pet professional has a similar skill set to you, doesn't mean you have to work with people in exactly the same way.

It's your business – you make the rules!

We need to be open to the idea that anything is possible, and that you can work with pet parents in any way you desire. You just need to believe that this fact is true for you.

Many of my clients first come to me with more traditional business models. Many are dog trainers who run in-person classes or one-to-one programmes. Some of them are dog walkers who offer group or one-to-one dog walks. Others are pet sitters offering daily pet visits and overnight stays. I've worked with vet physiotherapists who offer one-to-one rehabilitation services for their clients. I've supported dog groomers who offer grooming services. All of these pet professionals have one thing in common: They trade their time for money. They actively deliver a service for each client, in exchange for a set fee.

I'm not knocking this way of working. Many of us thrive when we're engaging with other humans and animals face-to-face every day. Being able to help other people and pets is probably the reason you started your business in the first place. However, the one-to-one model puts a cap on the amount of people you can serve and the amount of money you can make. Sure, you can increase your prices. That's one way to make more money without adding to your workload. You could also hire a team to help you serve more people, too. However, the added work and pressure of managing a team might not be where you want to take your business. There starts the dilemma: "How can I earn more and work less?"

To become a truly limitless pet business owner in income, impact and freedom, we need to think outside the box. That doesn't mean you have to do away with all the services you currently offer. You may, however, be inspired to let go of a service you've been thinking about dropping for a while now. It might inspire you to tweak a current service to make it work better for you.

You may feel excitement about setting up a new revenue stream that works alongside your current offerings. Or this might be the nudge you needed to totally pivot and change everything about the way you work with your ideal customers.

So, let's look at all the different business models that are available to you so you can start thinking about which one most aligns with you.

One-to-One Model

One-to-one may be your primary business model right now. You might be offering your services to pet parents in person, through email, by phone or video calls.

Here are a few ways that you might position your services to work with your clients within this category.

One-offs

You invite people to book in and pay for a single session or appointment with you. For example, you might be a dog groomer offering grooming appointments on a pay-as-you-go basis. Or you might be a dog trainer offering single one-hour training sessions for a set fee. This way of working is the least attractive option of any service you could offer. It means you need to be constantly looking for new clients to fill your calendar. Not ideal.

Packages

You create packages that include a set number of sessions at a set price over a certain period of time. Packages can be based on providing a very specific result or transformation for your client, or they might offer a way for your client to save a little money by buying in bulk. Either way, it encourages your client to commit to a longer-term relationship with you. For example, maybe you're a dog behaviourist and have a separation anxiety package with nine sessions over three months. Or perhaps you're a vet physiotherapist and your package offers six treatments over six months. Packages are more attractive as they bring recurring revenue into your business. It means you don't have to constantly source new clients to make the money you need.

Rolling Monthly

Lastly, you can set up a rolling monthly agreement your client pays until they decide to cancel. This works brilliantly for services that are needed on an ongoing basis. It gives you the security of consistent, long-term income where you can automate payments coming into your business. For example, maybe you're a dog walker and your client pays you every month for a set number of walks. Or your client pays for a set number of pet visits each week.

One to Many: Group Model

Instead of working one-on-one, the one-to-many group model means you can offer services to more people at the same time. This allows you to start impacting more pet parents and earn more for doing less.

Group Classes

Programs and classes can be offered in person or online. These can be offered as one-offs, packages or a rolling monthly service. For example, you might be a dog trainer and have 10 spots available on your six-week puppy programme. Each class is 60 minutes and you charge £165 per puppy. That's £1,650 for six hours of work. Now we're starting to create leveraged income that you can comfortably scale and make a more-than-decent living from. Or take it online and have no cap on the number of people who can join. Your earning potential just went through the roof!

Group Workshops

Again, workshops can be offered in person or online. Similar to classes, you bring a group of people together in an interactive environment to help them get the result they want. For example, maybe you're a dog walker who has a keen interest in adding enrichment to walks, or you might hold a workshop in your area that teaches other dog parents how to add more fun and enrichment to their own walks.

Live Challenges

An experience you take a group of pet parents through to help them achieve a specific result. They pay anywhere from £7 to £47 to get involved. You run the challenge over five days. Each day you teach them a step they can learn and you give them a quick task to complete. For example, you're a dog groomer and your challenge helps schnauzer owners groom their dogs at home. From nail clipping to teeth cleaning and coat maintenance.

Live Events

You hold in-person or online events. Whether that's to help pet parents overcome specific challenges or problems, or you organise meetups to help others connect. For example, you might be a pet first-aid specialist and organise an event for 40 people at a local hotel. Your event educates dog parents and other pet professionals on what they need to know in an emergency. Or maybe you're a dog trainer and you hold meetups for puppy parents to socialise their puppies and connect with like-minded people.

One to Many: Passive and Semi-passive

Here's where things start getting really interesting. This is how you can create an asset for your business that's infinitely scalable, and you can sell over and over again with little input from you. I've gone all in on passive and semi-passive income as my chosen business model. This is how your pet business becomes limitless in income, impact and freedom.

Online Courses

You take what you already know and turn it into video lessons and resources people can buy and consume online when they need it. You pick the biggest problem your clients face right now, and position your course as the solution to fix that problem. For example, you might create an online course with a step-by-step guide on how to groom a poodle at home. It could be an online course that teaches people how to get their dog to come back to them when called, or how to have stress-free walks with their dog. The options really are endless. Just start brainstorming.

E-books

This is a relatively simple and quick way to package up your expertise so you can sell it online. Your e-book helps people overcome a problem they're experiencing with their pet. Depending on how comprehensive that e-book is, you might sell it for anywhere between £2 and £20. You pull together the information and design and pop it up on your website where people can buy it at any time.

Recorded Workshops and Masterclasses

If you're not quite ready to create a course, this could be a good passive income option for you. It can be a simple 60-minute video on a specific topic. You might have a supporting worksheet or PDF to go with that to help your customers implement what they've learned. This option can be pretty quick to pull together. I've personally created and had masterclasses ready for sale in just a few hours. It doesn't have to take months of your time!

Workbooks, Diaries, Calendars or Checklists

Maybe you already have handouts and worksheets you offer your in-person customers that you could offer for sale. Or maybe there's a resource you could quickly pull together that could be useful for many more pet parents. For example, perhaps you're a dog trainer and you create a dog-training calendar with times and exercises that also allow them to track their dog's progress.

Bundles

This allows you to package up several different online resources and sell them as a bundle. This is a great option when you have lots of different online offerings and you want to drum up more sales with a special offer. You might offer three of your courses for the price of two. Or maybe they get your workshop and workbook as a bonus when they buy your course. When sales have stalled, bundles are a great way to encourage new interest.

Memberships

Now, we're stepping into the realms of semi-passive income. Online memberships give you a healthy dose of monthly recurring revenue. You invite people in and they pay you on a monthly basis to be a member. You might have some self-study video training and resources as part of your core curriculum. You might offer ongoing support in the form of a private community and live Q&As every month. You might release a bonus resource every month, too. It's semi-passive because there is a little work involved along the way if you're offering support and monthly resources.

Programmes

Programmes are similar to a membership, but rather than being ongoing, you take people through an experience together for only a set period of time. For example, you might offer a three-month separation anxiety programme. As part of the programme, there are core training sessions that unlock each week, which everyone learns from and implements at the same time. You'll likely offer support inside a community and on live calls, too. After three months, support ends and the experience is over.

I want you to be as in love with the work you do as I am. I never want you to feel burnt out because the spark has died, you're overworked and you're too scared to look at your bank balance. The knowledge that's stored in your brain is valuable. People deserve to be able to access it – it's selfish to keep it locked away! You deserve to be paid well for that knowledge, too. You should never have to feel in lack and like there's never enough money. It's in your power to make more. You just need to get smart about how you work with your ideal people. I hope this chapter goes some way towards showing you what's possible for you.

Pricing Your Services

Now that you know how you want to work with your people, we need to pin down what you'll charge. Many pet pros I speak with tie themselves in knots and second-guess their pricing all the time. If that's you, chill! This doesn't need to be complicated.

There's one crucial point I want you to take away here though: Never set your prices to be the cheapest. That race to the bottom is a game you're never going to win. You'll only end up burnt out and resenting the monster you've created.

Sure, it's a great idea to research the market to see what your competitors are doing and charging. That's just good business practice. However, we're not using that research to see how we can undercut others. We use it to understand how we can offer the very best service so we can charge a decent or premium price.

I want you to create an extraordinary service, own your worth and know that there are pet parents out there who are more than happy to pay for it. They exist – you just have to believe they do first.

There's no hard and fast rule to set your prices. Literally every business owner is making it up. A good place to start is to consider what you need to do to live the lifestyle you want. If you want to make £10K a month, start with the number of clients you're able to comfortably serve each day. Then consider how much you'll need to charge each client to ensure you hit that goal. This is a simple way to work out the right pricing for you.

Always price your services on the transformation you provide. Not the number of hours you put into it, not the features they get. The results and outcomes you give your clients are where the real value lies. Your services literally change the lives of pets and their people for the better.

Whether you're giving a dog some much-needed boredom relief and their owner peace of mind with your walking service, or you're helping a dog be calm and happy at home on their own, your behaviour work gives the owner their life back.

You're changing lives. That transformation is valuable and should never be underestimated. It's your job to ensure you effectively communicate that value to convince your ideal customer to buy.

What's most important is that your pricing feels energetically good for you. When someone buys from you, you should feel fantastic about the level of service you're going to give that person and the money you'll receive in return.

If it feels heavy, or you have thoughts around it not being worth your time, that's a big sign your pricing is out of alignment and it's time for an increase.

When considering your pricing, you can also ponder on these three criteria to help you come to the right figure. You should set your pricing:

- To ensure your ideal customer is able to see the true value in your offering.
- To ensure they will fully commit to the process and show up as your five-star ideal customer.
- To ensure you feel well compensated for the services you provide.

Now how do you feel about your pricing? Stretch yourself. How does it feel to push that price a little higher? How about a little further than that? Does it feel exciting, maybe even a little scary? That's OK. One of the best things you can do to start your journey towards limitless growth is to create a highly sought-after service you love delivering – and price well for it.

Exercise: Defining Your Aligned Services

In your workbook, make a list of all the services you currently provide in your pet business. Next to each one, rate that service on a scale of 1-10 based on how much you enjoy delivering it – 10 being you're in love with the service, 1 being you hate it. Look at the services that are marked with an 8 or lower, and consider which services you should drop or change in some way to make them work better for you.

While you're here, consider any new offerings you might like to add in, based on the list I've shared with you above. Then, use the guidance above to help you set your super-aligned pricing.

Grab your workbook below.

www.karlyedwards.com/workbook

Chapter 5
The Mothership of Your Business

Every business needs a virtual home. A place on the internet that people can visit and learn all they need to know about you and how you can help them. That place is your website, a.k.a. the mothership of your business. We need to have an online shop window that showcases you in all your magnificent glory. It still amazes me when people say they don't need a website for their business. Or they don't make it a priority and whip together something that looks like a five-year-old had a go.

There are so many benefits to having a solid website presence, and I'm not saying you need to shell out thousands of your hard-earned money to create one. However, we do need to ensure we have a home on the internet where people can visit, learn more and buy from us.

I see many pet professionals giving over control of their business presence to someone else. They'll create a Facebook page and see it as the job done and that's good enough. Or, they'll sign up to one of those sites that allow people to find professionals in their area. They're fine knowing that's the only virtual home they have. That's worrisome because if these platforms decide to change something or shut down, your business might go down with it.

I hate to burst your bubble if that's you too, but if you don't have a website, it can throw up question marks in your client's eyes around the seriousness of your business. There's a higher level of professionalism that comes with having your own website. If you're here reading this book, I know you're serious about growing your business. I know you're here to make a real difference in your life and the lives of others. For your customers to take you seriously, you need to give them the confidence in you that having a website presence brings.

Ultimately, our job is to drive as many people as possible to our website so they can make a buying decision. Having a website can do so much heavy lifting to sell your services for you. It allows you to show up in Google search so you can attract the right people to you without effort. It means you can direct people in your marketing to a specific place to learn more.

Then, when they get there, you wow them with your content and present them with an offer they can buy immediately. Having a clear and professional website can remove the need for those time-consuming call and email enquiries. Instead, you show them how amazing you are and what you offer, and give them a way to buy now.

Websites don't have to be complicated. Actually, keeping it simple and streamlined is the best way to make sales. So, let's break that down into a basic website that will work for you.

Home Page

Your home page is the page the majority of your visitors will see. It's where most people will enter your website, and sometimes exit immediately too. That's why we need to make it as enticing as possible, to encourage people to explore other pages and learn more about us. Your home page header is a great place to display a lovely picture of you and your pets, along with your power statement.

Remember the power statement we pulled together in a previous chapter? That goes here. Your home page shows your visitors they've come to the right place. This is where you speak to their biggest problems and desires. Draw them in by showing them you understand.

You should also link to some of your most popular services here, too. Then sprinkle the page with lots of lovely testimonials to instantly solidify your credibility.

About Me Page

Despite what you might think, your "About Me" page is not about you. Huh, what? It's about your customers and how you, as the expert, can help them get what they want. While you should talk about your experience, your values, your qualifications, your results, the awards you've won and your reason for being, you must tie this back into your customers and what's in it for them. Why does it matter to your customer that you have five qualifications around dog behaviour? Why does it matter that you have a 95% success rate in helping dogs with reactivity? It matters so they can have confidence that they're working with the most qualified person who's going to get the results they want, right?

With everything you share on your About Me page, always bring it back to how it's going to make your customer's life better.

Services Pages

Every single service you offer needs its own designated sales page. We don't want to cram everything you offer into one confusing page. Give each service the attention it deserves so your customers can make an informed buying decision. There are big benefits to structuring your website in this way.

First, Google is all about relevance. It wants to give its users the best results for their specific search query. When you separate your services into individual pages, each one is more likely to be ranked higher in the search engines. You're able to target relevant keywords more powerfully and give each page its own focus to convert visitors into customers.

The second big benefit is qualifying your customers. Individual service pages allow you to go deeper into the solutions you provide and give your potential customers everything they need to know. You can speak to their needs, tell them exactly what they're going to get and answer any questions they may have right on your sales page. This can remove the need for frustrating back-and-forth emails or long-winded calls, as your website does the heavy lifting for you.

10 Key Elements for Your Winning Sales Pages

There are 10 key elements you need to pay attention to when structuring your sales pages for the best results:

1. **Headline**
   Your headline should hook your visitors in immediately by spelling the solution out for them. Here you should focus on the result or transformation your service will help your customer achieve.

2. **Images**

    Capture your visitor's attention with a standout header image that relates to the service. Then include more images to support your content and break up your text further down the page. Ideally, include images of you working with pets rather than stock images.

3. **Problems**

    Speak to your visitor's biggest pain points. Describe the specific challenges that show up in their daily lives and show you understand. Show them you know exactly how they feel so they know they've come to the right place.

4. **Desires**

    From highlighting their problems, transition into painting a picture of their desired life. Speak to the big dreams they have for their life with their pet. Focus on how their life will be when their problem has been resolved.

5. **Benefits**

    Introduce the solution you offer and list out three to five big benefits of your offer. Talk about how your service is going to make their life better in a tangible way. It's things like: you'll be able to walk your dog without stress or embarrassment. You'll get your freedom back to live your life knowing your dog is settled at home on their own. Or you'll be free to entertain guests in your own home without your dog causing chaos. Get clear on the results they can expect to achieve by working with you.

6. **Features**

    Features are the details of your offer and what they'll actually get when they buy. It's the particulars like: You'll get three 60-minute sessions in my purpose-built dog training field. You'll get handouts to support you in implementing the training at home. You'll get email support on Thursdays from 9am to 5pm. It's everything you include in your service that your potential customer needs to know about.

7. **Why you?**

    Share the details of who you are and what you do. Let them know why you're the best person to help them get the results they want.

8. **Testimonials**

    Social proof is essential for helping you solidify your credibility. It helps your visitor feel confident in working with you. Sprinkle testimonials from your happy clients throughout your sales page.

9. **Price and call-to-action**

    Make the price of your service clear and include a button where they can take the next step, either to book a call or buy now. You should also sprinkle your call-to-action buttons throughout the page to give people plenty of opportunities to take the next step.

10. **FAQs**

    Include the common questions people often ask you at the bottom of the page. This can help remove some of the objections your visitor may have about getting in touch or buying now.

Contact Page

Your contact page has an important job to do. We want to make it easy for potential customers to get in touch with you, in whatever way you want them to do that. You set the rules here too, so think about how you want people to be able to get hold of you. I made a decision a few years ago to remove my phone number from my website. Getting random phone calls out of the blue does not bring me joy. So for me, I invite my visitors to send me an email to enquire.

You do what works for you. It's a good idea to include an inviting picture of yourself, your preferred contact information and some opening text that invites them to get in touch. Integrating a contact form into the page is a great way to make it easier for your visitors too. If you're a local business, it's good practice to integrate Google Maps into the page to help with SEO.

It's also a good opportunity to invite people to check out other important things you want them to know about, like how they can connect with you on social media or any freebies they might want to sign up for. This is the bare basics and structure of a solid professional website that will serve you well.

There are also a few "good to have" pages you might want to consider too:

Freebies page. A place where all your brilliant free resources/lead magnets live, that people can pop in their email address to grab. Lead magnets are a great way to grow your email list, and we should be making a consistent effort to grow it. The more leads you bring into the business, the more money you make.

Blog or podcast page. We'll be delving deeper into core content in the upcoming chapter, but having a blog or podcast page is a great way to demonstrate your expertise. This is where visitors can learn more about the topic you're knowledgeable about, and where you can form a deeper connection with your potential customers. This is what can help establish you as the pro you are.

Reviews page. Give all your amazing reviews and testimonials a home on your website where visitors can binge-read. It shows others that you've got results for your customers and helps them feel confident in working with you too.

If you don't already have a website, I hope this has helped you see how essential a website really is for your business. I hope with the above structure, you also feel clearer about how you can very simply lay out your own standout website. If you already have a website, I'm sure this has given you some useful tweaks you can do to make it even better.

Exercise: Creating Your Website

In your workbook, start fleshing out the individual pages that will make up your website. Under each one, include some bullet points that will guide you in creating the content you'll use on these pages.

Grab your workbook below.

www.karlyedwards.com/workbook

Chapter 6
Online Marketing Simplified

Now that we have your incredible website in the bag, we want to put it to good use and direct lots of lovely visitors to it. Remember, your website is the mothership of your business. Our job is to ensure as many people as possible have a chance to see it so they fall in love with what we're all about. To do that, you need a marketing strategy.

Your strategy needs to align with you and be as joyful and simple to implement as possible. I see too many pet professionals trying to do too many tactics at once, or doing things they hate, and it's just not sustainable. Inevitably they give up, which impacts their success and keeps them stuck. Marketing needs consistency. Whatever your strategy looks like, you need to be able to stick with it for the long haul. Consistently following an aligned strategy over many years is what built the successful business I have today.

Over the years, I've developed a unique approach to marketing called The Marketing Hive Method. Think of your website as a beehive. It is the central hub of your business. The job of the hive is to send out lots of busy bees to collect pollen that can be turned into delicious golden honey. In business, we send out our own worker bees by using specific tactics that bring pet parents back to our website, which we can then turn into customers and cash. In both examples, it's abundance galore!

The first step involves optimising all the profiles of your existing online presence – mainly your social media pages. We want to leave breadcrumbs that will take every single person on a predefined journey with you and your business. When you optimise this journey, every potential customer that crosses your path knows exactly what they should do next, because you've laid it all out for them.

I see pet pros missing opportunities to get leads and sales all the time because they haven't optimised their profiles. Don't let that be you too! This is such an easy change you can make that will have a massive impact on the number of leads and customers you bring in.

Even if you're not actively engaging or posting to all the social platforms, it's always a good idea to optimise them anyway, so you can point people to the best place to connect with you. Now, let's dig into how to optimise those social profiles, shall we?

Facebook (Personal Profile)

Despite what some "marketing gurus" tell you, I do advocate using a personal Facebook profile for business. Back in the day, Facebook would have frowned upon doing this and may even have shut your profile down. These days, Facebook is more relaxed about profiles being used for a mix of personal and business use. They even introduced the option to convert your profile into "professional mode." This gave us all the big green light from Zuckerburg. The reason I use and recommend using your profile for business, is mainly because profiles offer better reach than business pages and Facebook groups. It allows your content to be seen by more people. We all know how frustrating the algorithms can be for limiting our reach on pages and groups. Your profile gives you a gateway back into beating that.

Regardless of whether you decide to use your profile for business or not, we still need to optimise it. Because, as you interact with potential customers and sprinkle your magic on Facebook, they may hop over to your profile to check out what you're all about. If you haven't left those breadcrumbs for them, you've lost out on a new lead or customer. With that, here's how to optimise yours:

Profile picture. Include a clear headshot of yourself so people can get a better sense of the person behind the profile. Not your dog, a cause you support, a stock image or a funny quote you found somewhere. We want a nice picture of you smiling at the camera. Feel free to include your dog in the photo too. That's a great idea considering the industry you work in. People connect with people. People buy from people. Give them what they want.

Cover image. Your cover image is prime real estate. Use it to invite people to check out something important you want them to know about. You could showcase a freebie you have and invite them to sign up for it. Maybe you have an event coming up where they can join. Or maybe you just want to signpost them to your Facebook page or group. Use the space to direct people to where you want them to go.

Cover image description. Whatever information you've shared in your cover image, share more details about it in the description of that image and include the link where they can join or sign up.

Bio. Include a mixture of personal insight into who you are, and what you do in your business.

Link to business page. In the bio section of your profile, you can add a link to your Facebook page. If you have a page, we want to tell them about it. This is also where you can update your previous experience, links to your other social profiles and your personalised links to key pages on your website.

Personalised links. Highlight the most important pages your audience needs to know about on your website. This could be a link to your lead magnet, your core services, your blog or your free Facebook group.

Featured image. The featured image section is a great way to highlight one big thing you want them to do. For me, I have an image that showcases a particular lead magnet my potential customers can sign up for.

I understand that you may be hesitant about using your profile for business use. You may have been using it purely to connect with friends and family up to this point. I get that, I used to do this, too. The way I get around this is by using custom lists. On Facebook I've created a specific list for friends and family. Then, whenever I want to share a business post, I can exclude my friends and family from that post. That way, only my business-related contacts see it. I keep my profile public and don't mind everyone seeing my more personal posts. However, if you really don't want your business contacts seeing your personal posts, (because you're sharing photos of your kids or other sensitive content) you could create a list for all your potential customer friends too. Then, just exclude that list from any personal posts you share. There are ways to keep things separate if you really want to.

Facebook (Business Page)

Over the years, our reach on Facebook pages has dwindled dramatically. While this is incredibly frustrating, it always helps to optimise. You never know who will come and check you out. I personally don't put a whole lot of effort into my Facebook page. It's not the primary way I like to engage my audience. Sure, I repurpose and schedule content to go out each day and I've optimised the page to tell people what to do next. However, I probably spend less than 10 minutes a week paying any attention to it at all. Our time and attention is often best spent elsewhere. Again, our job is to leave breadcrumbs to show your visitors what to do next.

Profile picture. Add either a nice headshot of yourself (if you're a personal brand) or your logo (if you're a larger business with a team).

Cover image. Similar to your Facebook profile, use this space to invite people to do something specific. You might invite them to check out your lead magnet, a Facebook group or a core service/product.

Cover image description. Include more details about your lead magnet, group or service and why people should sign up, then include a call-to-action and the link where they can join.

Bio section. Share an overview of who you are, what you do and who you help. You could use the power statement formula you created in Chapter 3 here. It's also a good idea to include information about your lead magnet and a link where they can download it here, too.

Pinned post. Create a pinned post in the featured section to welcome people to your page. Pair it with a clear picture of you and your own pets, or your team if you have one. Welcome people to your page and briefly share what you do and how you help your people. Then, include the details of your lead magnet and a clear call to action to sign up.

Instagram

Whatever your feelings towards Instagram, there's no denying it's a great place for pet business owners to connect with pet parents. Instagram is a visual platform, and people love sharing pictures of their pets. In fact, according to a study by Statista in the UK in 2023, over half of pet parents post about their pets on social media at least every two days. With over 16 million homes in the UK with pets, that's a lot of potential customers that are actively engaged on social media – with Instagram being one of the top platforms of choice. Even if you're like me and aren't exactly besties with Instagram, it pays to have a presence there regardless.

Profile picture. You can see the theme here – be sure to include a clear headshot of yourself.

Name. If you're using your name or business name as your username, there's no need to repeat it in the name area too. Instead, pick a descriptor to share what you actually do as this helps your profile get found by more people searching for the solutions you provide.

Bio. Break up your bio into bullets using emojis. Here you could share what you do, something more personal about you and a call-to-action to check out the link you've shared below.

Link. We want to send visitors to a place where they can explore more about us. If you can create a page on your website to add relevant links, instead of using a tool like Linktree, do that. It's better to send people directly to your website than someone else's. Include all your important links on the page. For example, your lead magnet, your offers, a link to book a call and a link to your blog, podcast or Facebook group.

Highlights. Use Instagram highlights like a navigation bar on a website. Showcase things like your core offers, testimonials, contact, about, lead magnets etc. You can do this by creating an Instagram story and simply adding it to highlights.

These are the three essential profiles I recommend optimising for pet business owners. Why? Because it's mainly where your ideal audience hangs out. If you've set up accounts on other platforms like LinkedIn, X (formerly Twitter) and TikTok, it's worth giving your profiles a quick refresh in a similar way too.

The 5 Pillars of Your Marketing Hive

The easiest way to be successful in marketing your pet business is by having a simple strategy that feels good for you. By setting a standard for the actions you take each day or week, there's no guesswork involved. You know what you need to do, when you'll do it and you take consistent action. That's the key here. Even when you don't feel like showing up, even when you're feeling beaten down because you're not seeing quick results, even when you've managed to come up with the millionth excuse about why you can't – you pick yourself up and you do it anyway.

There's no such thing as an overnight success. Those other successful pet pros that seem like they sprang up out of nowhere with their thousands of followers and active communities, they've likely been working behind the scenes for years trying and failing until they finally had their breakthrough. Focus on where you are and where you want to be, then do what needs to be done to get there. Never waste your time and energy comparing yourself to others.

You will experience bumps in the road. You will fail along the way. Sometimes, you may feel like packing it all in. That's totally OK. You're not alone and we all have these feelings sometimes. What sets you apart from those that ultimately fail is that you never give up. The most successful people in this world have failed again and again. They've simply reframed that failure as a necessary step in the journey and turned it into a positive. One of the reasons I'm where I am today is due to my bull-headed stubbornness to succeed. I am a Taurus after all! Giving up isn't in my vocabulary. It's simply not an option for me. If you have a calling to change your life and the lives of others, you have to be prepared to put in the work to get there. Even when you fail a bunch of times.

With that said, this isn't about running yourself into the ground while you're building your empire. When you focus on the right steps and cut out the rest that isn't serving you, that's how you can climb to the top without burning yourself out. That's why I teach the 5 Pillars of your Marketing Hive. All you need to do is choose one tactic from each of the categories below:

1. Core Content
2. Repurpose System
3. Traffic Driver
4. Nurture Container
5. Engagement Strategy

The 5 Pillars are the basis of a powerful marketing strategy. There are many different activities you can implement in each pillar, which is often where many business owners fall down. They try to do it all, then they get overwhelmed trying to keep up and everything starts falling apart. That's why we utilise the

Power of One. In each of the categories, you'll choose just *one* tactic to implement for at least 90 days. You'll test and tweak your strategy until it's running like clockwork. Only when it's working seamlessly and delivering results do you start adding other elements to your strategy. Or, until you've given it a fair shot for a few months and still aren't getting results. Then you should look elsewhere. To help you understand the 5 Pillars better, let's look at each one more closely.

Core Content

To instil deep confidence in your customer that you're the perfect person for them, they need to see that you're the expert. How do you do that? By showing up and sharing your knowledge about your area of expertise. When I say sharing knowledge, I don't just mean throwing up a social media post either. Core content is lengthier and more in-depth than your typical social post. It's where you deep dive into specific problems your ideal customers face, and you provide useful solutions to help them. This is what sets you apart from other pet professionals offering the same services you do. It's what helps you stand out and become the go-to expert in your field. Core content is usually created in one of the following ways:

Podcast. This is where you create regular audio episodes to educate your audience about specific topics. You could deliver them as solo episodes where you're chatting on your own. For example: "How to add more enrichment into your dog's daily life," or "What's best: Kibble or raw feeding?" Or, you can create interview-style episodes where you bring guests on to chat. This helps your potential clients get to know you, your expertise and how you can help them.

Video. Similar to podcasting, but in a different format. You share videos that are insightful and informative for your audience on a regular basis. You might release them weekly, bi-weekly or monthly. The frequency depends on what works for you and how fast you want to grow. Having a YouTube channel works really well for this.

Blog. Again, a blog works in a similar way. You write regular articles on your website that offer insights and solutions around certain topics you specialise in. This is a great option if you're more confident writing rather than presenting. A blog isn't as effective as podcasts and videos at building those deeper relationships, as it can lack that intimacy and personal touch. However, it is great for search engine optimisation and helping you boost your website's rankings.

Most business owners miss this crucial step in their marketing. They focus on churning out superficial social media posts and wonder why it's not working. Core content gives all of your knowledge and brain magic a home. A place where your ideal customers are notified of your expertise on a weekly or monthly basis, and where they can binge-consume your greatness in one sitting.

This supercharges the getting-to-know-you phase and makes it easier to nurture your fans and convert them into customers. Remember, we're not looking to pursue all the core content formats right now. Just focus on the one that most aligns with you.

Repurpose System

Trying to think up new ideas for content all the time can be exhausting. It's a good idea to spread your message far and wide across multiple platforms, but we don't want it taking up so many hours of your time each week. That's where a repurpose system comes in handy. You can take one piece of content and spin it into many different formats, so you're not trying to reinvent the wheel each time.

The process for your repurpose system will be unique to you. It depends on what your marketing strategy currently looks like, or will look like when you've adopted the Marketing Hive Method. It's another reason why creating core content is so useful. You think up one big idea, then you can splinter it off and make at least 20 other pieces of content. I'll use my repurpose system as an example so you can understand how this could play out in your own business.

Step 1: My system starts with my podcast. Each podcast episode is automatically transcribed using software and turned into a blog post for my website.

Step 2: I'll take the show notes from my podcast episode and tweak them for a Friday email that gets sent to all my email subscribers.

Step 3: I'll use a template to design a quick image for the podcast episode, use the show notes for the caption and share it on my Facebook page, Instagram and LinkedIn.

Step 4: I'll use that same image to share a story for Instagram and Facebook, inviting people to check out the latest episode.

Step 5: I'll pull out paragraphs or poignant sentences from the blog post and use them to create around 20 posts for social media.

This is what I do and it feels good and easy for me and my team to implement. Your repurpose system may look a little different depending on what you choose to do. You could repurpose this even further though. Let's say you decide your core content will be video. Well, you could upload your regular videos to your YouTube channel. At the same time, using the audio for a podcast. Then take the transcription for a blog post. That way you've created one piece of content, but turned it into three different core content formats.

However, if you're just starting to introduce core content into your business, save this more advanced repurposing until a later stage. For now, just pull together a simple repurpose system you can rinse and repeat.

Traffic Driver

Remember our main goal in business: to drive traffic back to your website so your visitors can learn more about you and make a buying decision. Traffic is the lifeblood of your Marketing Hive. That's why we need a whole step in our strategy that allows us to do that. There are many different tactics you can use to drive traffic, but again, bear in mind the Power of One. By doubling down on just one traffic driver you'll be able to give it your full attention and get better results in the long run.

When considering the traffic driver you'll choose, always keep in mind your personality, energy levels and any budget you have to play with. If you have more money than time, one of the quickest ways to grow is with paid ads. If you have more time than money, organic marketing is the way to go.

Let's consider your traffic driver options in more detail:

Paid ads. Whether you're using Google, Facebook or Instagram, paid ads can be an effective way to pull people back to your website. The real beauty here is the hands-off nature. When your campaign is set up and converting well, it ticks over in the background, delivering you a steady flow of traffic and leads.

Organic social media. You can drive traffic simply by sharing content on your social media pages and regularly including links to your website. The key here is to share engaging content with a call to action in your posts. Focus on the one social media platform that you both enjoy using and get the best results from.

Groups and forums. Your ideal customers are actively hanging out in specific Facebook groups and forums right now. You can drive traffic to your website by sharing valuable content with links to your website, or by answering people's questions. This is where your core content can really shine. You can respond to people's questions by inviting them to check out a specific blog post, video or podcast episode you've created that will help them solve their problem.

Search engine optimisation (SEO). If your website doesn't rank highly in the search engines, you might want to turn your attention to SEO. By optimising your website for specific keywords your ideal customer is already searching for on Google, you can attract lots of qualified traffic for free.

Guest appearances. Being a guest expert for other people's audiences is a great way to grow your fan base and drive traffic. Think collaboration over competition, always. You could write a post for another business's blog. You could appear on their podcast or in their Facebook community. The idea here is to provide value first, then invite them to connect with you further. You could mention a free resource you have at the end or invite them to check out a specific service you offer.

Public relations (PR). By appearing in online publications, newspapers, magazines and TV regularly, you can open yourself up to whole new audiences. You might set yourself a goal to get PR coverage once or twice a month across different mediums to drive traffic back to your website.

Nurture Container

We need a space where you can nurture a much deeper relationship with your ideal customer. A place where your people feel special and like they're part of your business family. Having a nurture container creates a sense of intimacy with you – the person behind the business. It's how you can encourage meaningful conversations with the people that matter to your business. This goes beyond having static social media pages where it often becomes a one-way conversation. A nurture container creates a whole new level of closeness and familiarity between you and your ideal customer. There are two main ways you can create a nurture container: either through an email list or a Facebook group.

Email List

If you're not already growing an email list for your business, now is the time to start. If you don't have a nurture container yet, I always recommend starting with email. There are three main reasons for that.

1. Email is easier to manage long-term when you get everything set up.

2. Your email list is yours. Compared to social media, it's the only platform where you have complete control.

3. It typically gives you a higher ROI than many other marketing strategies.

Email gives you a direct line to get in front of your ideal customer. Think about it this way: According to research by Mailerlite[1], the average email open rate in the animal care and veterinary sector is around 45.79% in 2024. Social media reach, on the other hand, is more like 2 to 4% of your following, according to Socialinsider.[2] With these figures, you'd be crazy not to make email marketing a priority. With email, your audience is far more likely to open and read the content you've poured all your love and attention into. As they've actively opted in to get onto your email list, your subscribers are also far more likely to buy from you when you put an offer in front of them.

Here's one of the great advantages of email: You can segment your audience based on their interests and wow them with relevant and useful content on a regular basis. It enables you to build an engaged container where hundreds, even thousands of pet parents look forward to your emails.

I've been in business since 2013. I didn't start growing my email list until year six. If I could start all over again, I would have made email marketing my number one priority. So many other business owners I speak with say the same thing. At the time of writing this book, email is where over 70% of my leads, income and customers come from. More interestingly, my revenue growth is directly tied to my list growth. The bigger and more engaged your list, the more revenue you make.

The best way to grow your email list is by offering useful resources for your ideal audience. This is what we call a lead magnet, opt-in or freebie. You provide this resource for free in exchange for your audience's email address. It could be a short e-book, guide, checklist, template, calendar, planner or video training.

The options are endless. The key to getting sign-ups is giving your audience a resource they really need. This is why knowing your ideal customer deeply is so important here. You need to position your lead magnet as the painkiller solution to your people's biggest problem. Then, after they've jumped onto your list, you automatically nurture them with regular emails. This allows your subscribers to get to know you, your expertise and the solutions you provide.

Facebook Group

Growing a Facebook group is the second option for a nurture container. This is typically an option I'd recommend adding in after you have your email strategy in place. It gives you another space online to build and nurture those connections. With a group, you can build trust and credibility while you warm up your members for your paid services. It's one of the best places to create an active community around your business.

You could say email is a must-have and a Facebook group is more of a nice-to-have. However, there are plenty of big benefits to growing a Facebook community, though it can require more effort on your part to keep growing and engaging your members. Particularly in the early stages when you have less than a thousand members, it takes an almost daily commitment to post interesting content that will encourage members to interact.

If you do have time for that commitment, a Facebook group can be a powerful way to nurture and convert your members into customers. To make it worth your while, you need a strategy behind you before you jump in. Otherwise, you could run the risk of creating a ghost town. We've all seen those groups before. Or possibly even worse, running a group that takes up all of your time but gives you nothing in return. You need to strike a good balance so your group members don't just see it as a place for free support.

From the outset, they need to see that you do run a business. They need to understand that, while they will get a ton of value by being in your group, you do have services to sell, too. That's why you should never shy away from talking about what you do and how you can help.

To keep my group engaged, I post daily content that offers a mix of entertaining, educational, engaging and inspiring posts. To give my engagement a big boost and convert my members into paying customers, I also run live masterclasses, challenges and boot camps on a monthly basis. Live experiences can be a very effective strategy for free Facebook groups, not just to supercharge your group's engagement, but to turn those leads into people who buy from you. It gives you a platform to show up, give value and demonstrate your expertise, while at the same time, it presents them with an irresistible offer to buy and take the next step with you.

Engagement Strategy

Perhaps one of the most important parts of your Marketing Hive is your engagement strategy. By interacting and having conversations with your ideal customers every day, you can grow your audience, relationships and client base. Coming back to the Power of One – we want to choose just *on*e place where you'll spend time engaging with your audience. To find that perfect place, consider these three questions:

1. Where do your ideal clients hang out the most?
2. Where are you getting the best results right now?

3. Which platform do you enjoy being on the most?

Ideally, we want to choose the platform that scores highly in all three areas. Not only will you get better results, but you'll be more likely to stick with it because you enjoy it, or at least, don't mind it. By taking the time to interact with your ideal customers, you instantly become more human and relatable. People are far more likely to follow you and work with you when they feel they know you.

Remember that saying, "People buy from people." That's also why it's essential you show up as yourself when engaging online. Bring all your personality, humour and nuances to the table. Don't try to edit yourself too much or tone anything down. Let it out and show your audience the real you.

Authenticity is what people connect with.

The beauty of an engagement strategy is it allows you to reach more pet parents outside your existing audience. This isn't just about interacting with people who leave comments on your social media pages. (Although you should do that, too.) This is about finding your ideal people online and joining in the conversation. So, how can you do that?

Facebook Communities

One way you can do that is by leveraging other people's Facebook groups where your ideal customers are hanging out. To keep this from getting out of hand, choose the five best groups you can find and become the expert there. You do that by showing up regularly and providing value. You can use the search bar in groups to find relevant conversations happening around your expert topic. Then, leave an insightful comment that will help them with their problem. Of course, you can also share your own posts with value and top tips too. Just be sure to stick to the rules of the group. By doing that regularly, you'll soon become noticed as the go-to person for the work you do in these communities.

Hashtags

Another option is to select and follow five relevant hashtags on Instagram or X (Twitter) and engage with your ideal customer's posts. You can use the search bar on both platforms to find good hashtags. This will give you a list of many posts from people using that hashtag. All you need to do is leave an insightful comment and strike up a conversation with that person.

Share Quality Content Regularly

One of the great ways to get yourself out there and encourage engagement is to simply share quality content your audience needs to hear. If you've done your business basics work, you should have no problem creating content that will resonate with your ideal pet parents. If you want people to engage with your content, tell them that. Finish your social media posts by asking a question to start the conversation. Ask them to leave their thoughts in the comments. Sometimes, you just need to tell people what you want them to do next.

Conversations create relationships. Conversations lead to more sales. We need to make engaging part of our daily routine. For you, that might mean you schedule 30 minutes at 9am every morning to follow your engagement strategy. Interacting with pet parents is how you can expand your reach and further establish the know, like and trust factor in your ideal customers.

Exercise: Creating Your Marketing Hive

In your workbook, capture your own Marketing Hive. Remember to choose just one tactic from each of the five categories: Core Content, Repurpose System, Traffic Driver, Nurture Container or Engagement Strategy. This will create a strategy that allows you to stand out online and attract the pet parents you want to work with.

Grab your workbook below.

www.karlyedwards.com/workbook

Chapter 7
Being Visible on Social Media

Social media may be a big part of your marketing strategy. It is for many pet business owners, and why not? Social media allows you to promote your pet business and get in front of your audience for free. Before the 2000s, the only way businesses could market themselves was to pay for advertising. We're lucky to be running businesses in this new technological world, where social media exists and gives us the opportunity to reach many people across the world.

Having said that, this next confession may surprise you. I don't like social media. I'm a social media marketing expert, but as a super introvert and someone who naturally likes to keep to themselves, social media doesn't bring me a whole lot of joy. It's exactly why I teach pet business owners how to get better results in less time. So they can spend more of their time in the real world and less time having their mind digitally melted.

You shouldn't be spending hours of your time posting content to social media every day. It's easy to get sucked into drama, get triggered by the content you see or waste time doom-scrolling. We need to use our time wisely and follow a strategy to get the best results. No winging it and hoping something sticks.

Your Marketing Hive will come into play somewhat when you're pulling together your social media strategy. This includes the work you've fleshed out crafting your ideal customer and messaging. However, we need to go deeper into your content strategy and what you'll share. This starts with your Annual Content Plan. This will be your guide to ensure your content is strategic and intentional and supports your ultimate goals. We begin with the services you'll focus on selling throughout the year.

What Do You Want to Sell?

Every piece of content you share across social media should be intentional. It all needs to align with the services you want to sell. This is why we start by planning out which services you'll promote over the next 12 months. You might only have one service you want to sell, and that's totally OK. It actually makes your content strategy a whole lot easier. However, maybe you're a dog trainer and offer a range of different services. In this case, we want to think about when's going to be the best time to promote each service based on what your ideal customer needs.

For example, you might identify that in January, February and March, puppy classes are likely to be a big hit after many families welcome a new puppy into their home after Christmas. No matter how you feel about puppies as presents at Christmas, it happens. It's likely pet parents will need your help. Perhaps in April and May you want to sell your classes for adolescents.

Then perhaps in June and July when the warmer months come in and pet parents are looking for fun things to do with their dogs, maybe you focus on selling your scentwork classes. You get the idea. We need to have a solid idea of the service we want to sell first as that will guide all the content you share throughout the year.

What Are Your Content Themes?

From your promotion plan, now we need to consider the overarching content themes that will relate to the services we're selling. Using the same example above, from January to March, your content themes may simply be "puppies, puppy training tips, puppy care etc." You now know that all the content you create during these months must fall under these themes.

Now we're starting to form a content strategy and bring more purpose to our marketing. We do this because it allows you to attract and nurture a relationship with the right people, which are pet parents who will be interested in that topic and service.

Plus, it establishes you as the expert and the go-to person to help them solve their problem.

What Are Your Content Ideas?

It's time to get more granular and flesh out some of the subtopics you'll talk about each month. This will help you pull together a loose content plan for the year. Sticking to the puppy training example, some of your subtopics for January may include:

- Tips on socialising a puppy
- Puppy life skills
- Force-free training techniques and viewpoints
- Tips before you bring a puppy home
- Case studies and testimonials from happy customers
- Stories from your own puppy challenges and how you overcame them

Don't overthink it. Draw on your existing knowledge, your viewpoints and who you are as a business.

Your content ideas will give you a good guide on the types of content you'll share to create interest in your business and the services you offer.

The 8 Content Pillars for Social Media

This is an approach to creating social media content that I developed after a few years of struggling with my own content strategy. Using these pillars helps you categorise your content into buckets, making it far easier for you to follow a well-rounded social media strategy. What we don't want to do is fall into the trap of sharing the same types of content to your channels day in and day out. That can leave your profiles feeling stagnant and your engagement and results can dwindle as a result.

Let's take a dog groomer as an example. Over the years of working with many groomers, I've seen their entire content strategy made up of before and after pictures. Just streams of posts of the dogs they've groomed. Or dog trainers that post picture after picture of their clients holding certificates and rosettes after graduating from their classes. Or alternating between pictures of them working with their clients and posts that say, "Buy my thing!"

All of these types of posts have a place in your content strategy, but they shouldn't make up your entire strategy. We want to post a mixture of content types that serve to inspire, educate, entertain and convert. That's where my content pillars come into play. This is how you keep your feed fresh and your audience coming back for more.

When you plug these pillars into the way you share content on social media, suddenly it all feels a little less daunting. You'll have a clearer idea of the type of post you need to share each day, saving you time mindlessly staring at the blinking cursor of death. Let's dig into what these 8 Content Pillars are:

1. Story Posts to Build "Know, Like and Trust"

Story posts let people into the person behind the business. They allow your audience to get to know you on a human-to-human level. This is important because it strengthens the bond between you and your potential customer. It shows them, on an emotional level, that you are the perfect person for them. Don't be afraid to be vulnerable and let people into your world. Share those stories about your passions in life and why you do what you do.

Let people see your life with your own pets so they can get to know you and relate to you. Talk about what you got up to that day or over the weekend. Share your work and life experiences and how they relate to what you do today. People are naturally curious and want to know more about you. Don't deprive them of that.

When many of my clients first come to me, they lack the confidence to talk about themselves and share photos of themselves. I do get it. I used to have the same fears about putting myself out there, too. However, if you want to reach the heady heights of success you know you're capable of, you have to drop the ego and focus instead on being of service to the people who need you. Deeper connections, more opportunities and more success await you on the other side when you can overcome your fears of being visible. I promise you that.

2. Promotional Posts to Call People to Action

As the title suggests, these are posts specifically to promote a service you offer. I often come across two types of pet business owners. There are the ones who overdo it and go hard on the sales posts every day. Then there are the ones who rarely talk about the services they offer. There needs to be a healthy middle ground here. Don't forget to ask for the sale. You need to show your audience exactly how you can help them. You need to be painting a vivid picture of what life could look like when their problem is solved. Show them that you have the solution to get them there and include a clear call to action where they can learn more and buy now. It's that simple. You're in business to help people and make money. You won't make sales if you don't talk about what you do regularly.

3. Connection Builders to Show You Understand Them

As humans, we like to feel connected with other people. Before we make a buying decision, we also like to know that a business understands our current problems and desires. It helps us know we've come to the right place. With Connection Builders, you're putting yourself in your audience's shoes and showing them you understand where they are right now. In your content, you're speaking to their problems, challenges and desires. You're showing them you have a deep level of understanding of what matters to them.

Maybe you create a post to show empathy for your ideal customer because their dog is bouncing off the walls and they're struggling to get any work done at home. Maybe their dog barks constantly when they're left alone and it's causing a rift with the neighbours. Or maybe they're embarrassed and stressed out when they take their dog for a walk because they're reactive. Go all in on the details of those challenges and desires and tap into how it makes them feel.

4. Tips Posts to Share Value

As someone who is passionate about pets, you likely have vast knowledge of your expert field. We want to share that value with your audience to establish yourself as a knowledgeable and useful resource. Create content that will help your audience solve specific problems. Share quick tips they can put into action and get a quick win. It's not difficult, just take snippets of what you already know and create a post around that.

Maybe you're thinking, "Hold on Karly, if I share my knowledge for free, nobody will want to pay me for the work I do." I've heard this complaint a lot, but no, that never happens. It's impossible for your ideal customer to get everything they need from a single social media post. There will always be pet parents who want to save time on grooming or walking their dogs themselves. There will always be people who need a dog trainer or behaviourist who will give them the right techniques in the right order and someone to hold them accountable. That's why you have paid services. There will always be a need for you and the service you provide.

Be generous with your knowledge. It's only going to solidify you as the go-to person for the work you do.

5. Opinion Posts to Build Your Authority

If there's one content pillar most pet business owners avoid, it's this one. We often fear sharing our viewpoints and perspectives because we don't want to get backlash from others in the industry. We're scared of getting nasty comments, being called out as a fraud or getting cancelled. You can't let other people have control over you and your success. By sharing your opinions you'll become a magnet for your ideal customers.

The people who are a perfect fit for your business will be more drawn to working with you. We're not here to create content for your peers. They don't pay your bills. Don't be afraid to share the causes you stand for or the things that tick you off in your industry. Share your thoughts around what matters to you and watch as more pet parents flock to your corner of the internet.

6. Testimonial Posts to Build Credibility and Social Proof

Get into the habit of shouting about your successes and the results you've achieved. This is what gives other people the confidence to invest in your services. Create posts that include kind words you've received from your clients. Share case studies that talk about the problem a customer once had and what their life looks like now you've helped them solve it. Share your clients' incremental wins along the way. Celebrate your clients' achievements regularly to show others the results you facilitate and what it's like to work with you.

7. List Builders to Grow Your Email List

We should always be making an effort to grow our list. We don't want to rely solely on social media as a way to grow and communicate with our audience. Reaching your potential customers in their inbox gives you a more effective way to connect and nurture a deeper relationship. A great way to do that is to tell people why they should get on your list in the content you share. Give them a reason to join by offering a free resource that solves a specific problem. In the posts you share, talk about what your free lead magnet is, why they need it and how they can sign up for it.

8. Engagement Starters to Foster Interaction

Social media is primarily a platform to engage and interact. It's easy to lose sight of that sometimes when we're using it to promote our businesses. We can sometimes fall into a one-way broadcast situation. However, we want to encourage engagement and conversations, as this is what creates a sense of community around your business.

There are lots of ways you can create more engagement, from asking simple questions and running polls, to sharing GIFs, funny pet memes and animal-related quotes. Engagement Starters can be quick to put together and give your audience an easy way to get involved.

Aim to share a healthy mix of posts from the different content pillars across the week. It's helpful to set yourself a weekly content plan to create a standard for your strategy. For example, maybe on Mondays, you know you should share either an Engagement Starter or a Story Post. Then maybe Tuesday is either a Connection Builder or a Promotional Post. What and when you post will depend on your posting frequency and what best aligns with you. Just ensure you're sharing a balanced mix to captivate and convert your audience.

Exercise: Creating Your Social Media Strategy

In your workbook, capture the following:

- The services you'll sell across the year
- Your content themes based on the services you'll sell
- Your content ideas based on your content themes
- A weekly content plan that incorporates the 8 Content Pillars

Grab your workbook below.

www.karlyedwards.com/workbook

Chapter 8
Achieve More in Half the Time

I'm a lazy business owner. I'm constantly seeking out easier, quicker ways to do everything in my business. Productivity is a big part of what I teach – the more productive you are, the quicker you can grow. It also means you can spend less time faffing, and more time relaxing, which gets a big thumbs up from me.

Sometimes, we can overcomplicate business and take the difficult path, either because we can't see a better way, or because unconsciously, our belief system holds us back with thoughts like, "You have to work hard for your money." This limiting belief held me back in my business for years, until I finally realised there are much easier ways to grow and make money.

Now, in everything I do, I ask myself the question, "How can this be easier?" Try it for yourself when you come up against anything in your business that feels difficult or time-consuming. This simple question will prompt you to look for and implement alternative solutions that will make your life easier.

By introducing clever processes and systems into your business, you can create more freedom in your life. You'll stop doing those mundane tasks you hate and take you hours to complete. You'll reduce the overwhelm around always having so much to do. You'll be able to take time off when you want to and know your business is operating like clockwork. You don't have to do absolutely everything yourself, and you shouldn't. This kind of mentality will only limit your growth and what you're truly capable of achieving.

The "Do, Drop, Delay, Delegate, Systemise" Method

When you first consider how you can make things easier in your business, adopt the "Do, Drop, Delay, Delegate, Systemise" method. Not only will this help you prioritise the most important tasks in your business right now, but it'll help you see opportunities to streamline your business as a whole. This is how you can make crucial decisions around how you manage your time, so you can more efficiently achieve the goals that are important to you.

Do

Any tasks you place in the "Do" category are urgent and important, and you should take action on them immediately. These are often tasks that are tied to your most important goals. These tasks are your number one priority right now to ensure you hit that goal.

For example, if your goal is to hit £5K this month, but you can see you're falling short, your priority tasks might be to send follow-up emails to those who have enquired to work with you in the last few weeks. It might be to reach out to past customers and invite them to book your maintenance package, or maybe to strike up a conversation with 10 warm leads in your audience to see if you can help. Here you prioritise the actions that will have the biggest impact on your ability to achieve your ultimate goal.

Drop

These are tasks that are neither urgent nor important and should be dropped from your current schedule. They're often tasks that waste your time or distract you from other more important tasks in the business.

For example, maybe every week you have a team meeting or meet up with a business friend for a coffee. Maybe you have great intentions to discuss growth strategies, but it's never quite as useful or productive as it should be. Or maybe you spend hours creating and sending summary reports to your clients after their dog training classes, but nobody ever reads them. Or perhaps you're creating videos every day for TikTok but it's not actually bringing you any leads or customers. Consider where you're spending time and energy that isn't worth the effort, and remove those tasks from your to-do list.

Delay

Any tasks that are important but not urgent can be placed in the "Delay" category. You put these tasks on pause and schedule them when you have availability again. We can all get distracted sometimes by new ideas that pop into our heads, or we see something interesting online that we now feel we need to adopt or implement.

Ever heard of the term Shiny Object Syndrome? It's when we constantly get distracted by new opportunities we think are worth pursuing, which draw your attention away from those important priority tasks. Sometimes these ideas and opportunities are worth pursuing, while others are just a distraction. For both old ideas that aren't urgent and new ideas that spring up, jot them down in your Delay pile while you focus on those priority tasks first.

Delegate

Generally speaking, any tasks that are important but don't require your personal involvement should be delegated to someone else. This frees you up to focus on other areas of the business where you can operate in your zone of genius. You're a powerful force of nature, but you're still only human. There's only so much you can do. Outsourcing mundane tasks is one of the easiest ways to start delegating so you claim back more time.

For example, you might hire a Virtual Assistant (VA) to handle enquiries coming into your inbox. You might get a social media manager to post content on your behalf. Or you might hire an accountant and bookkeeper to manage the financial side of your business. If you're not making the money you want right now, I know hiring help isn't always doable. You can start small though. I started building my team with a VA who worked one hour a week to manage my inbox, schedule my social media content and engage in my Facebook communities. Delegate what's feasible in the beginning and grow from there.

Systemise

There has never been a better time to run a business. The technology and tools that are available to us today have revolutionised the way we can and should do business. Don't fear technology, embrace everything it can do for you. By systemising and automating certain aspects of your business, you can completely eliminate many time-wasting activities that are impacting your growth. For example, get a booking system so you can avoid time-sucking back-and-forth emails with customers. You could set up a payment system so customers can pay you through your website instead of sending invoices and having to chase payments all the time. You could use an email marketing platform to easily keep in touch with your customers and subscribers. Or you could use a social media scheduler so you're not manually posting to social media every day.

There are many smart tools you can introduce that will save you hours of wasted time every week. This could be time better spent either acquiring or serving your customers or enjoying some much-deserved downtime.

Standard Operating Procedures (SOPs) and Clever Systems

It's incredible how quickly day-to-day operations can take over if you're not careful. By introducing smart processes and systems, you can save many hours of precious time every month. You'll make your business more efficient and streamlined, so you can focus more on setting the stage for your limitless growth. A Standard Operating Procedure (SOP) is simply a document you create that outlines the exact steps you need to take to complete a specific task. There are lots of SOPs you can plug into your business to massively increase your productivity. You can have standard processes for things like:

- Customer sales
- Onboarding and offboarding new customers
- Customer communications
- Customer complaints
- CRM management
- Sales pipeline management
- Billing
- Service terms and conditions
- Creating and organising social media content
- Email marketing
- Creating blog posts
- Creating video content
- Creating podcast episodes

You can and should have a standard for the way you do almost everything in your business. It not only reduces the time you spend doing tasks, but it creates uniformity and ease for anyone else carrying out tasks on your team. Let me just cherry-pick a couple of examples from my business so you can see how you could apply systems and SOPs to your own.

Onboarding and Offboarding Customers

People can buy all of my offerings directly from my website. It's a smart move to have a payment system set up on your website to allow this too. Say, for example, they buy my signature programme. When they do that, they're automatically sent a welcome email with all the information they need to get started. My email system will then send another few emails to remind them to check out all the awesome features they have access to.

This keeps them engaged and makes them feel supported and looked after. Seven days before their programme access is due to come to an end, they'll be sent another automated email inviting them to continue getting support where they can pay a special monthly fee. If they don't want to continue, they're then sent another email that thanks them for being part of the programme and invites them to fill in a feedback form.

The entire onboarding and offboarding process is automated to ensure they're fully looked after and have everything they need, without taking up my time. How can you automate your own onboarding and offboarding process to save time?

Creating and Organising Marketing Content

To avoid being stuck on a content creation hamster wheel, get into the habit of batch-creating your content. Create a bunch of social media posts a week or a month in advance. Create a month's worth of blog posts, podcast episodes or videos. Batching ensures you stay consistent and helps your content become more intentional and strategic, while also stopping you from being taken away from other more important tasks in your business day-to-day.

When it comes to creation, use a tool like Trello to help you plan, organise, write and store your content. One of the most useful things I ever created for my business is my content library. It's a place where I store every single social media post I've ever created. I have hundreds of ready-made posts that I can reuse and schedule again and again. On those days, when my creativity has fallen flat or I'm taking time off, I can dip into my library and schedule out two weeks' worth of posts in a few minutes.

Sales Process

Every business needs to have a sales process. It's the repeatable process you use to take someone from stranger to customer. It should be a sales journey you've perfected and is the same for each person, a process you could easily pass onto someone else in your team if you needed to. In my business, for example, I reach out to five warm leads every day. These are people who have already shown an interest in the business by interacting with my content or joining my free Facebook group. I'll reach out with a friendly message like:

> "Hey {name},
>
> Thanks so much for joining my Pet Business Support group. I hope you love it as much as I do!
>
> I'd love to hear more about your pet business and what you do. What goals do you want to achieve this year?"

After they've shared their goals, I'll ask a series of standard questions to learn more about them. I'll ask about the biggest thing that's standing in the way of them achieving their goals. I'll ask if solving this problem is a priority for them right now. Then, I'll talk about a solution I have that can help them hit their goal, and I'll ask permission to share the details. When they say yes, I share a link to the sales page for that offer.

Every person I speak with goes into my sales pipeline where I can keep track of which stage they're at on the buying journey. I check in with this every day and use it to strategically follow up with people who are in limbo. With every lead, we're looking for a definitive yes or no answer. Our job is to follow up multiple times until we get that answer either way.

I like to sell through direct messages on Facebook and that works well for me, but your sales process might be a little different. Maybe yours involves a discovery call and you take payment over the phone. Whatever it is, you need a standard for your sales process.

Customer Communications

It's handy to have standardised templates you can tweak when existing and potential clients reach out to you. This might be a structured reply you can edit when someone enquires about working with you. You could have a template for requesting reviews, and another for customers that need reminding to fill out forms or information.

Having templates and someone who can manage communications like this on your behalf can really take the pressure off. In my business, my VA has her own customer support inbox that she manages. The business has standardised templates we use for different scenarios to improve our efficiency. For example, we have standard replies for:

- When someone emails to say they've forgotten their login details for the online portal
- When someone wants to cancel their membership
- When someone reaches out to receive a copy of their invoice
- When someone asks specific questions about how to use a digital resource

Consider where you're writing lengthy replies from scratch each time. Then create templates you can store for future use to save time.

Creating a Standard Operating Procedure

Don't overcomplicate this. To create an SOP, all you need is Google Docs. This way you can easily create and share your documents with other people on your team, and save them in a shiny new SOPs folder. The structure for a standard SOP might look something like this:

- Title of your Standard Operating Procedure
- The purpose of the SOP and the task it will achieve
- The person responsible for carrying out the process for your business
- The person responsible for reviewing and updating the SOP
- The step-by-step process that outlines exactly how to carry out the task in bulleted format
- Any images, videos or flowcharts that will support the person in carrying out the task
- Any key contacts or links the person might need to help them successfully implement the process

You likely have many different repeated tasks in your business right now that you can create a SOP for. Spending time today to streamline the back end of your business will save you heaps of time over the years to come.

Embrace Technology and Systems

I don't know what I'd do without all the systems and tools I've plugged into my business. I'd probably be a lot more stressed out and overwhelmed! Technology is booming. There's a magical world of platforms and apps that can make your life easier. Don't dismiss technology even if you're a self-confessed technophobe. Get curious about how it can support you in becoming the limitless pet business owner you know you're meant to be. It will empower you to create more money, impact and freedom than you ever thought possible.

I'm constantly looking for tools I can introduce that will free up my time. Time is our most precious resource. If you're currently wasting time on carrying out menial tasks, you're losing money. It's time you could spend more wisely on having conversations and making sales. That money can then be used to reinvest into the business so you can become even more efficient and make more sales. To ensure your limitless growth, this is the mindset you need to develop. You'll forever stagnate in business if you hold onto an "I can't afford it" attitude.

Exercise: Increasing Your Productivity

In your workbook, write down all the tasks you do in your business on a daily basis. Then split the page into the 5 categories from the Do, Drop, Delay, Delegate, Systemise method above, and start organising those tasks into the different lists.

Look at all the tasks you've written down, and write a new list with those that you'll create an SOP for. Then take action!

Grab your workbook below.

www.karlyedwards.com/workbook

Chapter 9
Designing Your Ideal Life

You don't need my permission or anyone else's to create your dream life. You simply have to claim it. The only limits are your own imagination and your ability to accept that you are deserving of more. I want your life to become unrecognisable to what it is now, and in the best way. I want you to be, do and have everything you desire.

To create an overflow of abundance in your life, in income, impact and freedom. Do you believe it's possible? It is, with belief in yourself and the commitment to changing the path you're currently on. Remember the work you've already done on creating the big vision for your life and business? It starts here. Without the vision, we can fall into spirals of uncertainty and procrastination. We must know the reality we want to create, to give us the drive we need to take action towards it. When you know what you want, you can start taking micro-actions that will incrementally move you steps closer to your ideal life. Not tomorrow, a few months or years from now. Today. You can make small, hugely impactful changes, *right now*. Let's explore how you can do that in a practical way.

Your Working Hours

Let's imagine your ideal life consists of working four days a week, Monday to Thursday, from 10am to 3pm. However, maybe your current reality involves working six days a week and long hours over the weekend. That's a big difference from your ideal, and you're probably pretty frustrated about that. To work towards that ideal, you could start by deciding that you're no longer going to work on Sunday.

Now, you might be thinking, "But Karly! That's my busiest day, I couldn't possibly take that time off." Let me tell you, you *can*. You simply give yourself permission and make a decision that this is your new reality. Then, take care of the necessary logistics to make it happen. Like informing your clients of the change and no longer allowing people to book in on a Sunday. We can wrap ourselves in knots over decisions like this because we're too afraid of the negative consequences we create in our minds.

Those unhelpful mind monkeys that say you'll lose out on customers, or limiting beliefs that say you have to work a certain way if you want to make money in this industry. It's all BS. If you want to make a change that will support you in showing up as your best self so you can be the best for your customers, you can and should.

Boundaries, Boundaries, Boundaries

I know that you're in this industry working with pets and their people because you're compassionate and you truly care. You have a calling to make a positive difference, but that can sometimes be to your detriment. You might be a total people pleaser. Maybe you answer the phone to your clients at 9pm when you'd rather be relaxing with your own family and pets. You might often experience clients cancelling appointments last minute and leaving you out of pocket.

You might see clients pushing the scope or level of support that was initially agreed upon. Maybe your clients often become over-familiar and offload all their life problems onto you. Without boundaries, your personal and business life can become exhausting.

Without *clear* boundaries, you give other people free rein in how they can behave towards you. To avoid that, we need to set expectations with clients from the very beginning of the relationship. We need to share robust terms and conditions with them that they're required to sign. For your limitless growth, it's essential that you create and clearly communicate your boundaries with other people, and actively reinforce them when they're being pushed.

It's OK to Say "No"

Sometimes a client will come along that we know isn't a great fit for us. It might be something they say that sends up a red flag, like asking for a discount or having unrealistic expectations about the relationship. Always listen to your intuition if something feels off. Your instincts are often right. Even if you could really do with the money and you'd hate to see it go, the stress they create in your life is never worth it. You might come across opportunities in your business that seem like a great next step at the moment. But maybe you're swamped with other projects and work that are the priority to take you to your ultimate goals. Or maybe the opportunity seems interesting on the surface, but it doesn't fully align with your business values. Not every opportunity that comes your way is worth pursuing. It's OK to say no if it's not in your best interests.

The same applies to your personal life, too. If friends or family invite you to a party or to grab a coffee but you're feeling run down, don't feel guilty for declining an invite or having to rearrange. It's essential to take time for yourself when you need it. Your mental, physical and emotional health should always be your top priority.

Be Wide Open to Receiving Money

To have all the things that exist in your ideal life, you'll likely need money. There's no getting away from that fact. Whether you want a five-bedroom house in the countryside, three holidays abroad a year or a piece of land to hold your dog training classes. In many cases, we need money to make our big vision happen. Which means you must have a brilliant relationship with money. You need to be wholly comfortable with receiving money for the work you do.

You need to know in your heart that you offer an incredible service and deserve to be well compensated for it. You need to know that it's safe to create extraordinary levels of wealth in your life. Because it is. Any mindset blocks that may be stopping you from receiving more, you need to bring to the surface, explore them and let them go. If you've often struggled to attract and keep money in your life, you likely have money mindset blocks that need unpicking. Don't avoid the inner work. Overcoming your money blocks is essential for your limitless expansion.

Grow Your Savings Pot

For some people, growing their money isn't the big problem, it's keeping it. To have the things you want in your life, you need to be able to save and look after your money. I've always been a brilliant saver. My biggest problem was always releasing the purse strings and spending money.

It's probably because I've spent the best part of my life struggling to make ends meet. I'd squirrel away as much money as I could because I always thought at the back of my mind, "What if I don't make any more?" That was one of my own money mindset blocks I've had to overcome. Now, I know that money is energy and must flow like everything else in this world. Money flows to us, but it must also flow out and we should never be afraid to spend. There is always more money to be made. Remember that.

You can start small. When I first started saving money from my business, I'd put away just 5% of my income. As my business revenue has grown over the years, it's now much more than that. Even if it's just £5 a week, start somewhere. Whatever it is for you, make that commitment to save whenever you sit down to manage your money. Future you will thank you for it.

Making Small Upgrades

Even if your dream life feels lightyears away right now, small upgrades make a huge difference. Slowly but surely, you'll bring sparkles of that ideal life into your reality. This way, you'll acclimatise yourself to a new, better version of you. There may be many areas of your life that make you feel unhappy, low quality, uncomfortable or embarrassed. You may find there are plenty of life circumstances that you've been tolerating.

A small upgrade could be as simple as giving yourself permission to buy your favourite tea over the budget version. Upgrade your bedsheets that have become faded and itchy. Buying a pot of paint to brighten up the downstairs toilet that's started looking tired. Making incremental changes to your current life will move you another step closer to your ideal. It's time to stop tolerating what makes your life feel second-class. It's time to step into the future you that has everything she wants and needs.

Living the Ideal Life Now

Your mind is more powerful than you know. We have the incredible power to control our personal energy, thoughts and emotions in a split second. The key is in not allowing your emotions to have control over you, and realising that you are the conductor of how you feel. You can choose how you want to feel on any given day. You can choose to feel happy, successful and at peace right now. You might be thinking, "Yeah right, my life's a mess, what do I have to be happy about?" Let me tell you, I really do understand, because I've lived in negative thought patterns for most of my life. It took deep self-exploration to reach the levels of happiness and tranquillity I have now. Before you can experience the success, abundance and freedom you may want in your life, you need to start thinking, feeling and acting as if you already have everything you desire. Read that sentence again, it's important.

That means bringing into your consciousness and embodying the future you as you envision it, every single day. Tap into how that ideal version of you feels, and let those emotions wash over you. This is what raises your energetic frequency in line with everything you desire. If the future version of you has more money than she knows what to do with, look for signs of financial abundance that already exist in your life. Go on a treasure hunt around your home and put all the money you find in a jar where you can see it every day.

If future you feels accomplished, look at what you can tick off your list today to help you feel accomplished. If future you feels at peace, start by taking just two minutes to sit in the quiet with your eyes closed and breathe.

No matter how far away your ideal life seems, you can start living, acting and feeling as if you are already that person right now. That is what will pull you on the right track to achieving it faster than anything else can.

Exercise: Shaping Your Ideal Life

In your workbook, write down three incremental changes you can make this week that will take you one step closer to living your ideal life, then put them into action. See this as an ongoing process of small impactful changes that will steadily bring future you into your existing reality. Then, every day, anchor in and embody future you by raising your vibration while thinking, feeling and acting as her. Your ideal life is ready for you to claim it!

Grab your workbook below.
www.karlyedwards.com/workbook

Chapter 10
The Anti-Hustle Way

Remember that big societal belief that states, "If you want to be successful, you have to work really hard." This way of thinking has been drummed into us from a very young age. Your teachers or parents may have said this to you growing up. You may have witnessed your parents working all hours for the money they made, solidifying this belief within you further. Seeing my dad go to work as a bricklayer at 7am, seven days a week did that for me. This is why this belief was such a tough one for me to shake. The big difference now though, is that we have far more opportunities available to us. There are thousands upon thousands of ways you can make money.

I don't subscribe to the idea of hustling to hit the next big goal at all costs. I often see people in the business world getting so fixated on reaching their £10K months, then £20K, then £50K months, they're on a never-ending race to the top. They're working all hours, pushing like crazy to achieve more, be more, and have more at the expense of their mental, physical, emotional and spiritual health. Then they're surprised when they inevitably burn out. The pressure we can put on ourselves to achieve more can be immense. It's no wonder chronic health conditions are at an all-time high. Our nervous systems are fried and many people are just trying to survive day to day. Good job there's a better way – the anti-hustle way.

Choose Ease in Everything You Do

There are often so many different ways you can do anything in life. Some are convoluted and overly complicated, while others are straightforward and easy. Sometimes, when we're holding onto the belief that we have to work really hard to be successful, whether we're consciously aware of it or not, we overcomplicate our businesses to justify that belief. It's like we're proving it to ourselves, "See, it is true!"

Start questioning the way you do things in both your business and life. Ask yourself, is there an easier way to get the same or better result? Soon enough, all those actions you took to introduce more ease into your life will add up. Suddenly you'll realise you have more free time on your hands and you'll wonder why you didn't do it sooner.

Be Accepting of Support

I used to be so proud of being a strong, independent woman.

I still am. At my very core, I'm a raving feminist who deeply supports empowering women to be the best versions of themselves in this world. The major difference now is that I've learned it's OK and necessary to accept support on your journey to limitless growth. Empires aren't built by one person alone. We're not machines without emotion or an endless supply of energy.

Accepting support can be particularly tough for the women of the world. In a lot of ways, society expects us to be superhuman and to do it all alone. We're deemed the caregivers whose job it is to raise children and look after the home. At the same time, we're also expected to have successful careers. We should just suck it up and do it without complaining, too. I know there are nuances and things have moved on a little. However, we can't get away from the fact that the underlying patriarchy and everything that goes with it still very much exists today.

You have to get comfortable with asking for and receiving help. Especially if you want to reach your next level in business. Whether that's by hiring someone to support you in your business to plug a weakness or save you time, or getting help in your personal life. That might mean having a chat with your partner to discuss how they can take on a little more responsibility around the house. Or it might mean outsourcing help, like hiring a cleaner every couple of weeks, getting a supermarket delivery so you're not spending over an hour in the store on your day off or hiring a dog walker a couple times a week so you can focus on growing your business. Getting support makes your life easier and we should never resist it. It's essential not just to grow a wildly profitable pet business, but to keep your sanity on that journey.

Prioritise Self-Care

You can't show up in all your power if your energy reserves are depleted. Running a business is an emotional rollercoaster. When we don't give our minds and bodies what they need, everyone suffers. You, your immediate family and your clients are negatively impacted, which is why you have to get on board with regular self-care. It's not selfish to look after your own well-being. You're not a bad person if you want and need to do something for yourself. You are the most important person in your universe. Yes, even before your partner, your parents, your children and your pets. If you don't look after yourself and you're running on empty, you can't support other people to the best of your ability. There's a reason planes tell you to put your oxygen mask on before helping anyone else. You can't help anyone if you're dead. OK, that's a little dramatic, but you get the idea.

Self-care means different things for different people. What may feel good and energise one person, may be the opposite for another. What's most important is that you tune into your own individual needs and take action on them. For you, that may be taking a long hot bath without distractions every week. It could be giving yourself 10 minutes every morning to meditate. It might be morning yoga, going for a run or ensuring you're eating healthy meals five days a week. Or maybe you love music and you commit to seeing live music once a month to energise you.

In whatever way that works for you, self-care is purely about doing the things that make you happy and pulling energy back into your mind and body. Make it a routine and schedule it into your calendar so it becomes a priority.

One Step at a Time

While I talk about looking after yourself on your journey to limitless growth, you won't get there unless you take action. That's what sets you apart from those who stagnate to those who create the life and business of their dreams. You must take consistent action if you want to achieve your goals. Often when I first start working with a new client, they have no issue with motivation and taking action. These are my favourite types of clients. Their biggest problem is usually the desire to do everything all at once. You can't fault their commitment to succeed, but they slowly fall into the hustling trap. Staying up late, working all hours, pushing, pushing, pushing. Yes, sometimes there's lots to do to grow your dream pet business, but it's a process that can't and shouldn't be rushed. That's why having a plan and strategy is so important. It gives you the roadmap and timeframes in which you'll act on and achieve your goals. Consistent baby steps are how you'll get there. Working in alignment with your personality and energy levels is what creates a sustainable business. Just make sure you have fun along the way.

Final Words

We've come to the end of our journey together. If there's one big idea I want you to take away after reading this book, it's this: You are an extraordinary human being with gifts and talents that are desperately needed in this world. You have the power to make a positive change in the pet industry and greatly impact the lives of pets and their people. It's in your power to shape the pet world for the better while creating a business and lifestyle that's in total alignment with you. You can grow a hugely profitable, influential pet business that is easy and fun to run. You just need to have the right strategy in place and absolute belief and trust that it's possible for you.

I want you to start putting yourself out there with confidence so you can attract all the clients and money you desire. I want to see you making smart decisions about how you operate the back end of your business, and how you serve your valued customers to inject more ease into your life. I want this to be the day you start making game-changing shifts that will change the course of your life forever. It's time to take action and embody a new limitless you – in income, impact and freedom.

I'm so grateful you picked up this book and took the time to read it to the end. Thank you. I hope this book has inspired you to become the mightiest version of yourself and go after those big, beautiful dreams of yours. My hope is that you've come away feeling motivated to grow your pet business, your way, with the plan of action you need to make it happen.

I know you have it in you to create your limitless pet business. I know you're committed to creating a life of abundance in income, impact and freedom. You wouldn't have made it to the end of this book otherwise. The power is in your hands to change your existing reality for the better.

Now go get it! Dream it, and make it happen.

Your Next Steps

If you liked this book, please do share it with your pet business buddies. We're so much stronger when we're supporting and lifting each other up.

I've helped thousands of pet business owners create their easy, fun and wildly profitable pet businesses online. I'd love to help you do the same, and there are a number of ways I can support you through my signature programme Limitless Pets Academy, online courses, membership and resources.

If you're ready to create your Limitless Pet Business, please visit my website:

www.karlyedwards.com

Check out the Limitless Pet Business Podcast for more online business and marketing tips:

www.karlyedwards.com/podcast

Join the "Pet Business Support: Building Success Online" free Facebook group:

www.facebook.com/groups/petbusinesscontentmarketing

Limitless Pets Academy

The best place to get support from me is through Limitless Pets Academy. This is my 12-month online programme that will take you from the overworked, underpaid and overwhelmed pet business owner you are today, to unleashing the limitless you and growing a business you truly love.

The Academy supports female, ethical, service-based pet business owners who make at least £2,000 a month, grow their revenue exponentially while reducing their workload by at least 50%. Here's how the Academy can support you:

- You'll at least double your income with more ease

- You'll streamline your business and drastically reduce your working hours so you can have more time off to enjoy life
- You'll refine or expand your in-person services, while growing infinitely scalable online revenue streams
- You'll put your flag in the sand and become the number one choice for the work you do
- You'll embody unstoppable confidence and belief in yourself to create the business of your dreams

What you'll get inside the Academy:

- A powerful core curriculum with video masterclasses, tech tutorials and supporting resources to help you implement as you grow and scale your limitless pet business
- An exclusive online community to ask questions and get support when you need it
- A coaching call with me each month, giving you the guidance you need to make game-changing shifts in your business
- A reflection session with me each month where you'll get a peek behind the scenes in my business to draw inspiration for your own, and you can ask me anything

- 1-1 voice note and text coaching once a month. A chance for you to message me privately throughout the day to get those burning questions answered.

- Accountability pods with your fellow pet pros to keep you moving forward to achieve win after win

- Bonuses – practically done-for-you social media posts and content prompts to save time, get better results and take away the stress from your social media marketing

There is a criteria we look for in the pet pros we support. We don't accept everyone into the Academy, which is why we have an application process to enter the programme that I personally review.

To learn more about how Limitless Pets Academy can support you and to apply, visit:

www.karlyedwards.com/academy

About the Author

Karly Edwards is a certified business strategist and the go-to pet business coach. She helps pet professionals establish themselves as the number one pet expert in their field and make more money while working less. With her knack for simplifying business strategy, Karly instils belief and confidence in pet business owners, showing them they can achieve absolutely anything they set their minds to.

Karly is a self-confessed super introvert – a lover of crafting, gardening and soaking in the sun. She lives with her partner Chris and miniature schnauzer, Loki, in not-so-sunny Wales, UK.

Connect with Karly on Facebook:
www.facebook.com/TheKarlyEdwards

Connect with Karly on Instagram:
www.instagram.com/karlyedwards/

Website: www.karlyedwards.com

Reviews

"If you're a pet business owner looking to take the next step in growing your business, this book is a brilliant place to start. It's packed with practical, easy-to-implement advice on creating scalable income streams through online courses, memberships and social media strategies.

Karly's writing style is incredibly engaging, making what can feel like overwhelming topics clear and approachable. I actually read the whole book in one sitting – which is unheard of for me! And then I went back through it with a notepad and pen because her step-by-step guides ensure you know *exactly* where to focus your efforts.

For those unsure how to transition from trading time for money to building a more sustainable, scalable business model, this book is the perfect guide. I highly recommend it."

– Vicki Main, Dog Trainer at Love Your Paws Dog Training

"If you're anything like me, you know that running a dog training business isn't just about the dogs – it's about creating something that makes a difference in the lives of dogs and their humans. From the moment I started this book, I was hooked!

Karly has an incredible knack for breaking down complex concepts into bite-sized pieces that are not only easy to digest but also super engaging. Every word makes it feel like you're having a heart-to-heart chat with a friend who just happens to be awesome at giving business advice. You'll find yourself nodding along, thinking, 'Yes! This is exactly what I needed to hear!'

As someone who's passionate about supporting fellow dog trainers and the community at large, I can't emphasise enough how vital it is for us to share resources like this. Karly has poured her heart and soul into creating something truly special, and it's a message that deserves to be amplified far and wide. So, if you're ready to finally sort this part of your life out and make meaningful progress in your business, grab a copy of *Your Limitless Pet Business*. Together, we can raise the bar for our industry and create a community of thriving dog professionals!"

– Jo Moorcroft & Vicky Davis, Creative Business Strategists at Canine Business Academy

"I have been an avid listener of Karly's podcast for a while, so I was delighted to get my hands on her first book. It was easy to read and was packed with actionable advice that you can put into practice right away. This is going to be a great resource for our industry, and I eagerly await her next contribution."

– Salina Prescott, Dog Groomer at Doggy Furdoos

References

[1]Mailerlite, Duncan Elder, 2023, https://www.mailerlite.com/blog/compare-your-email-performance-metrics-industry-benchmarks (accessed 7 October 2024)

[2]Socialinsider, Charu Mitra Dubey, 2024, https://www.socialinsider.io/blog/social-media-reach/ (accessed 7 October 2024)

www.ingramcontent.com/pod-product-compliance
Lightning Source LLC
Chambersburg PA
CBHW070608010526
44118CB00012B/1471